Wine Country

Recipes

Revised Edition

Francis Publications
Fort Bragg, California

WINE COUNTRY RECIPES
Copyright © 1995 by Alan and Jeanne Francis

All rights reserved. No portion of this book may be reproduced by any means, for any purpose other than review, without the prior written consent of the publisher. For information contact:

Francis Publications
P.O. Box 1485
Fort Bragg, California 95437
Telephone 707-964-4193   Fax 707-964-5714

ISBN No. 1-886048-02-9

Published in the United States of America

Typography: Cypress House, Fort Bragg, California 95437

ABOUT THE COLLECTION

*T*en years ago as we stumbled along with Steppin' Out Magazine in the embryonic stages, we realized that the blending of fine wines and good food would be our main focus — and the collection began.

Over the years, the most common compliment from our readers has been, "Oh, we love the recipes in Steppin' Out!" So, we decided to celebrate our tenth anniversary with this fine collection of recipes.

The collection is a tribute to the people who live in the wine country and ply their trade in the food and wine industries — the real people who toil in fields and cellars, gardens and kitchens, to create the spectacular array of fine wines and excellent foods that are unique to our North Coast Wine Country.

WINE COUNTRY RECIPES is dedicated to my husband, Alan, who envisioned the concept and encouraged me to pursue the compilation of recipes. He will always be remembered for his creative ideas and love of life. He was, and remains, my inspiration.

From your publisher,
Jeanne Francis

WHAT THE CRITICS ARE SAYING ABOUT

BANDIERA

Bandiera has one mission: to produce the highest quality wine from premium appellations at a price that offers great value to the consumer. Here are a few critical reports on our success.

"Best Buys:"
- Bandiera Cabernet
  1986, 1987, 1988, 1989, 1990
- Bandiera Chardonnay
  1990, 1991, 1992
- Bandiera Sauvignon Blanc
  1993

- Wine Spectator

- The San Francisco Chronicle -

"I don't know how they do it up at Bandiera, but for several years the winery has made very good Cabernet and sold it at ridiculous prices ... The wine has more going for it than price alone: It's a richly flavored Cabernet with good varietal fruit character, well-balanced and pleasing."

- Larry Walker

- Food Arts -

It isn't just the wine critics who admire our wine:

"Napa Valley (Cabernet) doesn't have to mean expensive, even when it means very good wine. Here's a gem for the low end of the list, tasty and solid. Score: 86

BANDIERA WINES ARE DISTRIBUTED NATIONALLY
- VISIT OUR TASTING ROOM -
OPEN DAILY 10 - 4:30
8860 Sonoma Hwy. Kenwood
833-2448

CONTENTS

INTRODUCTION:
  WINE, FOOD AND NUTRITION VII

PART ONE:
  SPECIAL MENUS 1

PART TWO:
  APPETIZERS 13

PART THREE:
  BREAKFAST & BRUNCH 22

PART FOUR:
  SOUPS & SALADS 49

PART FIVE:
  ENTREES 65

PART SIX:
  DESSERTS 116

INDEX 139

LIST OF CONTRIBUTORS 144

TOUR THE TOWN OF
KENWOOD

in the beautiful Sonoma Valley

Explore our Wonderful Tasting Rooms, Be a Part of the Comraderie, Join us in our Seasonal Activities and Sample our Award-Winning Wines.

BANDIERA
8860 SONOMA HWY.
(707) 833-2448

KENWOOD VINEYARDS
9592 SONOMA HWY.
(707) 833-5891

CHATEAU ST. JEAN
8555 SONOMA HWY.
(707) 833-4134

LANDMARK
101 ADOBE CANYON RD.
(707) 833-1144

SMOTHERS WINERY
9575 SONOMA HWY.
(707) 833-1010

STONE CREEK VINEYARDS
9380 SONOMA HWY.
(707) 833-4455

We are Open Daily 10 - 4:30

KENWOOD, CALIFORNIA 95452

WINE, FOOD AND NUTRITION

*E*ver since grapes were first crushed and fermented, wine has been closely linked to food. Throughout history, wine has been enjoyed with other foods during meals. The California wine industry recommends the moderate, responsible consumption of wine with food in family or other social settings. Whether a jug of modest table wine or a bottle of rare vintage, wine is a rich beverage that not only enhances the flavors of foods but contributes energy, vitamins, minerals and other compounds to the diet.

Wine is the most healthful and hygienic of beverages.

Louis Pasteur (1822–1895)

Wine Complements Meals

Wine can add immeasurably to the pleasures of a leisurely meal with family and friends. It is a natural companion not only to the enjoyment of good food, but also to the relaxation and good conversation which help make a good meal memorable.

In Europe, wine has long been the beverage of both commoners and kings--as much a part of a rustic peasant lunch as of a regal banquet. Although wine is a newcomer by comparison to Europe, American winemaking skills and wine lovers' enthusiasm have more than caught up--especially in viewing wine as a complement to meals. After all, wine is a food and is at its convivial best when other foods accompany it.

In fact, a nationwide survey of over 1,000 wine drinkers found that 88% of those polled agreed that wine is the drink that goes best with food. The majority also found wine easiest to digest of all alcohol beverages and the preferred drink for a family in a restaurant.

A subsequent survey also found that wine was the alcohol beverage judged the most perfect complement to a special meal, as

Pairing Wine with Food

Wine Class	Best-Known Types		Wine & Food Combinations
Appetizer wines	Sherry Sparkling wines White table wines		BEFORE or between meals. Serve well chilled, without food, or with nuts, cheeses and hors d'oeuvres.
White table wine	Chablis Chardonnay Chenin Blanc Pinot Blanc Gewürztraminer Riesling	Sauvignon Blanc Semillon White Zinfandel Other blush wines	WITH lighter dishes. Serve chilled with chicken, fish, shellfish, pork, omelets, any white meat. Also served as an appetizer wine.
Red table wine	Barbera Grenache Cabernet Sauvignon Gamay Meritage blends	Merlot Petite Syrah Pinot Noir rosé Zinfandel	WITH hearty dishes. Serve at cool room temperature with steaks, chops, roasts, game—any red meat—cheese dishes and pasta. Serve Gamay, rosé and blush wines with all foods.
Dessert wines	Muscat Port	Late harvest wines	AT dessert. Serve chilled or at cool room temperature.
Sparkling wines	Natural (very dry) Brut (dry) Extra Dry (semidry)	Sec (sweet) Demi-Sec (sweet)	WITH all foods. Serve well chilled with appetizers, main courses or desserts.

well the most appropriate alcohol beverage to serve at celebrations such as birthdays or weddings. The bottom line is that most people who choose a glass of wine with their meals, whether at home or in a restaurant, do so because they enjoy the way it tastes. There is something exquisitely pleasant in the interplay of wine and other foods mingling across the taste buds that enhances even the simplest meal.

What Wine with what Food?

Pairing wine with food can be as simple as pouring a glass of what's on hand to go with whatever's in the refrigerator--or as complex as searching out every nuance in the vintage to bring out the subtle flavors in a gourmet meal. California's famed vineyards offer an amazingly wide range of fine wines with choices to suit every taste, every purpose and every pocketbook.

Part of the enjoyment comes from sampling and comparing wines to discover your favorites. Most people prefer drier wines with meals or appetizers and sweeter wines with desserts. But even experts admit there are no hard and fast rules.

Let your own personal taste be your guide. You are the sole authority on your palate. If you enjoy a wine and what it does with your food, you've found the right one.

The following suggestions are intended not as strict rules but simply as guidelines.

With appetizers, sure bets include chilled white wines or not-too-sweet sparkling wines or a dry sherry. (Lovers of red wine can even design a savory hors d'oeuvre tray around a glass of their own personal favorite.) For the main course, pour a dry table wine: white, red, rosé or sparkling wine. If you're serving a sequence of courses, it's usually best to start with lighter foods and wines and progress to more assertive ones.

In general, delicate foods such as seafood and poultry call for a delicately flavored white wine. Heartier fare, from pastas to roasts to full-flavored cheeses, can stand up to robust reds. For a good rule of thumb, the more highly flavored the dish, the more full-bodied the wine can be.

Cooking with Wine

Wine is not only famed for being good with food, but for being good in food. Professional chefs and enthusiastic home cooks all over the world know that even simple recipes can be elevated to elegance with a touch of wine.

Most of the alcohol evaporates during cooking but the wine flavors remain in concentrated form. The effect can be enhanced by serving the very same wine at the meal. Wine can find its way into foods in many ways. It can marinate meat and poultry, perk up sauces and stocks, mellow the flavors of soups and stews, and add sparkle to fruit desserts.

Wine Cookery Chart

These recommendations are intended as suggestions. Many experienced cooks add wine entirely by taste, just as they do salt. Use these amounts as rough estimates when flavoring each dish.

	FOODS	AMOUNT	WINES
Soups	Cream soups	1 or 2 teaspoons/ serving	Dry white wine, sherry
	Meat and vegetable soups		Dry white or red wine, sherry
	Bouillon or clear soups		Dry white or red wine, sherry
Seafoods	Fish and shellfish	½ cup/lb	Dry white wine
Poultry & Game	Chicken, broiled or sautéed	¼ cup/lb	Dry white or red wine
	Braised chicken	¼ cup/lb	Dry white wine
	Gravy for chicken or turkey	2 tablespoons/cup	Dry white or red wine, sherry
	Rabbit, braised	¼ cup/lb	Dry white or red wine
	Duck, roast (basting)	¼ cup/lb	Dry red wine
	Venison, roast (basting), stew	¼ cup/lb	Dry red wine
	Pheasant, roast (basting) or sauté	¼ cup/lb	Dry white or red wine, sherry
Meats	Beef roast, pot roast, stew	¼ cup/lb	Dry red wine
	Hamburger	2 tablespoons/lb	Dry red wine
	Steak, marinade	3 tablespoons/lb	Red wine, sherry
	Lamb and veal, roast, stew	¼ cup/lb	Dry white wine or rosé
	Lamb chops, marinade	2 tablespoons/lb	Dry red wine
	Pork, roast (basting)	¼ cup/lb	Dry red or white wine, rosé, sherry
	Gravy for roasts	2 tablespoons/cup	Dry red or white wine, sherry
	Ham (whole), baked (basting)	2 cups	Port, blush, rosé
	Pork tenderloin, sautéed	¼ cup/lb	Dry white wine
Cheese Dishes	Soufflés and other light dishes	½–1 cup/lb	Dry white wine
	Robust cheese dishes	½–1 cup/lb	Dry white or red wine
Egg Dishes	Scrambled, omelets, baked	1 teaspoon– 1 tablespoon/egg	Dry white wine
Sauces	Cream sauce and variations	1 tablespoon/cup	Dry white wine, sherry
	Brown sauce and variations	1 tablespoon/cup	Dry red wine, sherry
	Tomato sauce	1 tablespoon/cup	Dry red wine, sherry
	Cheese sauce	1 tablespoon/cup	Dry white wine, sherry
	Dessert sauce	1 tablespoon/cup	Port, Muscat, sweet sherry, sweet white wine
Casseroles	Meat, poultry, seafood, egg, cheese	1 tablespoon/cup of sauce	Use wine suggested for protein ingredient
Fruits	Compotes and fruit cups	2 tablespoons/ serving	Port, Muscat, sparkling wine, sweet white wine
Desserts	Puddings, cold desserts	1 tablespoon/ serving	Any dessert wine, sweet white wine, sweet sparkling wine

Wine in the Restaurant and Home Kitchen

Premium wines are a basic and often essential ingredient in many restaurant kitchens, where using several gallons each day--just for cooking--is not uncommon. Whether marinating a chicken breast in Cabernet Sauvignon, sauteing wild mushrooms in Chardonnay or dressing a salad with Champagne vinaigrette, wine is valued for its ability to make otherwise ordinary flavors zoom into the extraordinary.

Chefs who cook with wine do it for yet another reason--to keep the use of fats and salt to a minimum without compromising flavor. When wine is part of the poaching liquid, marinade, or stock, oils and butter can be used very sparingly. A tsp. of butter adds flavor, but a half cup as the cooking medium adds 700 calories--all from saturated fat. By comparison a half cup of wine is a fat-free 80-100 calories, and much of that evaporates before serving.

Making a small ensemble seem like an orchestra to the palate is one of wine's everyday culinary feats. This is possible because cooking concentrates wine's many aromatic compounds (natural tannins and flavors such as cinnamon, vanilla, citrus, etc.) into a 'liquid seasoning blend' that is low in sodium and high in potassium. Wine was most likely the first meat tenderizer known to humans. With today's renewed interest in leaner meats, we can enjoy the same properties of wine our ancestors discovered--its ability to soften or break down meat protein. This action is a function of wine's natural acidity and has the effect of making protein more digestible, requiring less time on the stove.

Which Wines for Cooking?

Any good premium wine can be used, either a varietal (i.e., wine from a particular grape, such as Zinfandel, Gewurtztraminer, Cabernet Sauvignon, etc.) or a blend (e.g., dry white or red table wines). Wines that have been opened and are not at their best for drinking may do very well for cooking.

Taste the wine first to be certain that it matches your culinary intentions. Top chefs recommend following these three keys:

- Use only wines you would want to drink.
- Cook wine long enough to evaporate the alcohol.
- Don't use too much or the acidity will overwhelm other flavors.

Cooking with wine is an opportunity for creativity and experimentation. Chicken in red wine or beef in Champagne can be unexpectedly delectable. Let your preferences by your guide.

For allowing us to reprint this article, we would like to thank:

The Wine Institute
Research and Education Dept.
"Wine & America"

DOMAINE CHANDON

Tour this exquisite French-owned sparkling wine facility and discover secrets of the traditional *méthode champenoise* style of winemaking. Enjoy a glass of Chandon sparkling wine with complimentary hors d'oeuvres in the salon or on the terrace.

Open 11 AM to 6 PM daily from May to October and Wednesday through Sunday, November to April.

Domaine Chandon Restaurant
★ ★ ★ ★ ★
Lunch and Dinner

For more information call (707) 944-2280

Restaurant Reservations: (707) 944-2892

California Drive, Yountville

SPECIAL MENUS

A feast is made for laughter and wine maketh merry.

Ecclesiastes 10:19

CARAMELIZED ONION TARTE TATIN
Philippe Jeanty, Domaine Chandon

6 small red onions
6 oz. French feta
6 sprigs fresh chervil
1/2 cup Balsamic vinegar
1 Tbsp. olive oil
Salt and pepper
2 medium leeks, diced, using white & light green part only
3 sprigs fresh sage
2 Tbsp. sweet butter
6 each 4 1/4" circles puff pastry

BLACK OLIVE FETA VINAIGRETTE
1/4 cup feta cheese, crumbled
1/8 cup cider vinegar
1 Tbsp. sherry vinegar
1/4 cup olive oil
1/4 cup extra virgin oil
2 1/2 cups shallots, chopped
Salt & pepper to taste
1/4 cup black oil-cured olives, chopped coarsely

Peel onions, place in baking dish. Pour vinegar over and drizzle olive oil. Season. Cook at 350 degrees covered for 45 minutes and uncovered for another 15 minutes, turning onions over from time to time. Set aside to cool, then dice.

Using a sauté pan, over medium heat, sear sage and thyme in the olive oil and butter. Add leeks and sauté slowly until leeks are tender, approximately 10-15 minutes. Set aside.

Line six 4" tart molds with parchment paper. Spoon a 1/3" layer of leeks. Cover each with a 4 1/4" circle of puff pastry (brushed with egg wash) and bake for 6 minutes in a 475 degree oven. When tarts are golden brown, turn each one over onto a serving plate so that the onions will show. Crumble 1 ounce feta on each tart, cracked black pepper and garnish with sprig of fresh chervil. Serves 6. Optional: Drizzle Black Olive Feta Vinaigrette around tart tatins.

SPICY FLORIDA ROCK SHRIMP RISOTTO
Philippe Jeanty, Domaine Chandon

In a large stock pot, heat olive oil over medium high heat. Add onion, cook for 3 minutes and stir with a wood spatula so the onions do not color. Add risotto, sage, thyme; cook another 2 minutes, continuing to stir. Add boiling chicken stock, 2 ounces at a time. Cook risotto for about 10 minutes until "al dente." Add shrimp, tomato, cayenne pepper, pancetta and Parmesan. Continue to cook, stirring the entire time until risotto is "al dente" and creamy.

Finish by adding basil, parsley, and sweet butter. Adjust seasoning and divide into 6 soup plates.

Serve immediately. Serves 6.

1 1/2 pounds Florida rock shrimp, peeled and deveined

6 oz. tomato concasee, peeled and seeded

1/2 oz. pancetta, julienned

3/4 oz. fresh parsley, chopped

1 pound Beretta risotto, superfino Arborio

1/2 medium yellow onion, chopped

2 quarts chicken stock

2 oz. "Regiano" Parmesan, freshly grated

1 1/2 oz. olive oil

3 oz. fresh sweet butter

4 leaves fresh sage

2 sprigs fresh thyme

1 branch fresh basil, julienned leaves

Salt and pepper to taste

RASPBERRY MILKSHAKE IN A CHOCOLATE BAG
Domaine Chandon

6 plain coffee bags with wax linings

2 lbs. Belgium dark chocolate (bittersweet couverture)

1/2 gallon vanilla ice cream (preferably homemade, or buy the best)

3 baskets fresh raspberries

3 oz. raspberry liqueur

1 cup milk

3 tsp. lemon juice

6 Peruvian lilies

6 fern tips

18 palmier cookies

6 straws

1 pair pinking shears

1 blender

1 small pastry brush

1 bowl with Bain Marie to melt chocolate

1 wooden spoon

Cut paper bags about 3 1/2" high with pinking shears. Open bags.

Chop the chocolate; place in a bowl and put the bowl over warm water. Melt the chocolate, stirring constantly with wooden spatula. When melted, take the bowl out of the water and keep stirring until chocolate cools down (about 10 minutes). Place bowl back over water for 5 seconds.

Pour the chocolate in each bag, about half way up. Turn the bags over, making sure that the chocolate coats sides of the bag. Let set in freezer or refrigerator until hardened; then with a small paintbrush "patch" the cracks and holes, if any (set back into freezer). Starting at the bottom of the bag, peel the paper off very gently. Reserve your chocolate bags in freezer.

In blender, place the ice cream (you may have to do this in 3 batches depending on the size of your blender), the raspberries which have been cooked for 15 minutes (sugar may be added depending on how sweet they are— you may use frozen raspberries if no fresh ones are available), the milk, lemon juice and raspberry liquor. Blend until smooth.

Place your chocolate bag in a plate. Fill 3/4" with the raspberry milkshake. Inside the bag, place a straw on one side, a flower on the other. In the front right side of the bag, place a tip fern, with a few raspberries in the top and 3 palmiers cookies in the front left side...and have fun!

PEAR SORBET
Philippe Jeanty, Domaine Chandon

Bring to a boil, set aside, and cool. Run pears through a Champion juicer. Immediately add lemon juice and syrup to pear juice. Pour into ice cream machine and process to manufacturer's instructions. Makes 1 quart.

Syrup:
2 cups granulated sugar
1 cup water

CHOCOLATE SORBET
Philippe Jeanty, Domaine Chandon

Bring all ingredients to a boil. Cool. Process in ice cream machine according to manufacturer's instructions.

This chocolate sorbet has a wonderful, rich chocolate flavor and sensual texture.

$4^1/2$ cups water
7 oz. Valrhona cocoa powder
17 oz. granulated sugar

A glass of wine is a great refreshment after a hard day's work

Beethoven (1770–1827)

Taste a Napa Valley Tradition

"Your sincerity, hospitality, and high standards of winemaking cannot be matched..."
Raymond Visitor, 1992

The family and staff of Raymond Vineyard and Cellar invite you to discover a Napa Valley treasure. Tour the winery and vineyard, browse in our retail room, and enjoy tasting current releases and selected library vintages with a staff specializing in hospitality!

Raymond Vineyard and Cellar
849 Zinfandel Lane
St. Helena, CA 94574
1.800.525.2659

MENU & SUGGESTED WINES

RAYMOND VINEYARD & CELLAR

Baby lettuce Salad with Prawns & Grapefruit
Raymond Sauvignon Blanc

Saltimbocca Alla Roma
Raymond Napa Valley Chardonnay

Poached Pears in Wine Cream with Raspberries
Raymond Late Harvest Semillon

BABY LETTUCE SALAD WITH PRAWNS & GRAPEFRUIT
Raymond Vineyards

Poach prawns in the wine with 1/2 of the herbs, until prawns turn barely pink. Remove from heat and let cool in the liquid. When cool drain prawns, reserving the liquid. Strain liquid into small saucepan and reduce over medium heat until liquid is about $1/4$ cup. Let cool and then whisk in olive oil until thickened. Add tarragon and salt and pepper as needed.

To assemble, place lettuce on 4 chilled salad plates. Arrange prawns and grapefruit in pinwheel design in center. Drizzle with dressing and sprinkle with the fresh chopped chives.

4 cups mixed baby lettuces, washed thoroughly & dried

16 medium prawns, peeled and deveined

16 pink grapefruit sections

1 cup Raymond Sauvignon Blanc

1 tsp. chopped fresh tarragon

1 tsp. chopped fresh chives

1 cup light olive oil

My manner of living is plain and I do not mean to be put out of it. A glass of wine and a bit of mutton are always ready.

George Washington (1732–1799)

SALTIMBOCCA ALLA ROMA

8 veal scallops
8 slices Prosciutto, paper thin
8 fresh sage leaves

Lay veal scallops flat on counter and top with one slice Proscuitto and one sage leaf each. Fasten together with a toothpick by making a "stitch" through all three layers. Melt butter over medium heat in a sauté pan. Sauté each scallop for 2 minutes on the veal side and 1 minute on the Proscuitto side. Transfer to a heated platter and keep warm. Pour wine into sauce pan and reduce over high heat for 2 minutes, scraping pan and stirring. Pour over veal and serve. Garnish platter with fresh sage bouquet.
Serves 4.

Wine is inspiring and adds greatly to the joy of living.

Napoleon (1769–1821)

POACHED PEARS IN WINE CREAM WITH RASPBERRIES

For the sauce, combine the 5 egg yolks with the sugar in the top of a double boiler and beat until well blended and pale yellow in color. Add the wine and whisk thoroughly. Cook the wine and whisk thoroughly. Cook sauce over simmering water, stirring constantly until it coats a spoon and begins to thicken. Do not let boil. Remove from heat and add the vanilla, lemon peel, and cinnamon. Chill for 1-2 hours. Fold in the whipped cream and chill 1 additional hour.

To assemble, cover bottom of dessert plates with the wine cream and place poached pear half in center. Pear can be sliced and fanned out, if desired. Top with 1 teaspoon of wine cream and surround pear with fresh raspberries. Plates can also be garnished with fresh mint leaves if available.

Serves 4.

5 egg yolks
1/2 cup sugar
3/4 cup Raymond Late Harvest Semilon
1/2 tsp. vanilla extract
1 tsp. grated lemon peel
Pinch of cinnamon
1 cup heavy cream, whipped to soft peaks
4 pear halves, poached in a light sugar syrup until barely softened
1 cup raspberries

Scharffenberger

SCHARFFENBERGER CELLARS, founded in 1981 by John Scharffenberger, is committed to the fine art of crafting ultra-premium California sparkling wines by the centuries-old *méthode champenoise*. The winery's mission is to produce sparkling wines that please the most discriminating wine drinker — sparkling wines which emulate the quality of the finest Champagnes, yet possess their own distinctive style. In recent years, Scharffenberger sparkling wines have been widely acknowledged as among the finest produced in America.

The house style is characterized by its non-vintage *Brut*: crisp and dry with a fruity, refreshing finish.

Scharffenberger Cellars also produces a vintage *Blanc de Blancs*, a vintage *Brut Rosé* and a *Crémant*.

VISIT THE WINERY IN ANDERSON VALLEY
SCHARFFENBERGER CELLARS
TASTING ROOM OPEN DAILY 11A.M. TO 5P.M.
8501 HIGHWAY 128
PHILO, CALIFORNIA 95466
(800) 824-7754 • (707) 895-2065

CURRIED CHICKEN BREASTS WITH RICE SALAD

John Schmitt, owner of The Boonville Hotel with his wife Jeanne Eliades, provided these recipes for SCHARFFENBERGER CELLARS.

Sauté breasts over low heat until just firmed up.

Transfer to baking dish.

Deglaze skillet with 1/4 cup white wine.

Pour over breasts, salt lightly, cover with foil.

Bake at 300 degrees for 15 minutes until just firm.

Loosen foil and allow to cool to room temperature.

Have ready 6 boned chicken breasts

In a large skillet combine 1/4 cup olive oil and 1/2 Tbs. curry powder

Rice Salad

Preheat oven and casserole dish to 350 degrees.

Prepare stock in hot casserole. Sauté rice and olive oil until heated through. Add to stock. Cover and bake for 15 minutes. Remove from oven, uncover and fluff. Let stand.

Mix vinegar and sugar and drizzle over cooling rice. Re-fluff.

Mound Rice Salad on a large platter, surrounded by a generous bed of cilantro. Place Curried Chicken Breasts around base. Condiments might include apricot chutney or fresh fruit salsa, nuts (pinenuts, toasted silvered almonds, peanuts), currants warmed in a little wine, avocado cubes tossed with lime juice, sour cream or yogurt, red onions in raspberry vinegar, toasted coconut and lime wedges.

Enjoy with a bottle of Scharffenberger Cellars Brut NV. Bon Appétit!

STOCK

3 1/2 cups water

Salt to taste

1 slice lemon

1 small chunk fresh ginger

1 clove garlic

1 sprig fresh mint

2 cups Basmati rice in 1 Tbs. olive oil

2 Tbs. rice vinegar

2 Tbs. sugar

When you visit Geyser Peak, you'll taste the wines that have set us apart from other wineries both in style and flavor.

Of course you'll also enjoy our beautifull hillside winery, our picnic area, our souvenir shop and views of magnificent Alexander Valley. Open daily 10-5. Located 85 miles north of San Francisco.

GEYSER PEAK

22281 CHIANTI ROAD, P.O. BOX 25, GEYSERVILLE, CALIFORNIA 95441   800-255-9463

APPETIZERS

You can't have a civilized meal without wine.

Julia Child

GOAT CHEESE CAKE
Chateau St. Jean

1 1/2 cups flour
1 stick butter
Pinch of salt
3 Tbsp. cold water

FILLING
12 oz. goat cheese, room temperature
16 oz. cream cheese, room temperature
3 eggs
1/2 tsp. each: fresh chopped rosemary, marjoram and thyme
1 tsp. chopped fresh parsley
1/2 cup pine nuts

Place crust in tarte pan and line with parchment. Fill with pie weights and bake at 350 degrees for 30 minutes.

Blend cheeses; add eggs one at a time. Add herbs. Fill crust with cheese filling; sprinkle with pine nuts and bake at 350 degrees for 30-45 minutes until firm. Cool to room temperature.

Recommended wine: Chateau St. Jean, Fume Blanc.

SPICY APRICOT-GINGER APPETIZER
Bandiera Winery

1 small jar apricot preserves
2 Tbsp. fresh ginger, peeled and chopped, or 2 tsp. ginger powder
1 tsp. red pepper flakes
1 8-oz. pkg. cream cheese
1 pkg. crackers

Combine apricot, ginger and red pepper flakes in a small mixing bowl. Unwrap cream cheese and place on serving dish. Spoon apricot mixture over cream cheese and serve with crackers.

Perfect picnic addition when served with Bandiera White Zinfandel!

SUN-DRIED TOMATO & CHEESE HORS D'OEUVRE
Geyser Peak Winery

Cut each piece of French bread into thirds. Place the bread under the broiler and lightly toast one side.

Pass the Mozzarella through food processor. Add the Ricotta to the food processor and mix. Season cheese mixture with garlic salt and white pepper.

Dry the sun-dried tomatoes on paper towels. Cut each tomato in half. Place a tomato on the untoasted side of the bread.

Evenly spread the cheese mixture over the bread, covering it completely. Top the cheese mixture with two capers.

Place the hors d'oeuvres under the broiler until the cheese melts. Serve immediately.

Preparation time: 30 minutes.

Yield: 2^1/$_2$ dozen hors d'oeuvres.

10 slices French bread
^{1}/$_2$ pound Mozzarella cheese
^{1}/$_8$ pound Ricotta cheese
15 sun-dried tomatoes, packed in oil
Dash garlic salt
Dash white pepper
1 Tbsp. capers

I feast on wine and bread, and feasts they are.

Michelangelo (1475—1564)

SEAFOOD IN PHYLLO DOUGH
Dehaven Valley Farm

1 pkg. phyllo dough
1/4 pound unsalted butter
8 oz. salmon filets, bones removed
6 oz. scallops
8 oz. bay shrimp
8 oz. red snapper filets, bones removed
4 Roma tomatoes, seeded and diced
1/4 cup fresh grated Parmesan cheese
1/8 cup medium Cheddar cheese, grated
1 cup loosely packed fresh spinach (torn leaves)
1 Tbsp. fresh squeezed lemon juice
1 tsp. fresh sage, finely chopped
2 Tbsp. olive oil
1 Tbsp. butter
1 Tbsp. Worcestershire sauce
1/4 cup shallots, diced
2 Tbsp. thinly sliced scallions (green part)
1/2 cup mushrooms, sliced
Salt and freshly ground pepper to taste

Cut fish into 1/2"–3/4" pieces, sauté shallots, mushrooms, and scallions in Worcestershire sauce, olive oil and 1 tablespoon butter. Combine all filling ingredients together; mix gently but thoroughly.

Following directions on phyllo dough package, place 1–1 1/4 cup filling in the center of a buttered phyllo sheet. Fold phyllo around filling in thirds, brushing with melted butter at each fold. Fold one end to the front, and one end to the back, ending with a rectangular package, approximately 3"x7". Makes 6 "packages."

Bake in preheated 350 degree oven for 25–30 minutes until phyllo dough turns golden brown.

Rice pilaf and steamed broccoli make nice accompanying dishes.

Note: *Approximately 2 pounds of any combination of fresh fish and seafood can be used in place of those suggested.*

MACCALLUM HOUSE MUSHROOMS
Alan Kantor, MacCallum House Restaurant

In a heavy saucepan, sauté garlic in 1 teaspoon butter. Add wine, cream cheese, sour cream, and chopped mushrooms. Cook over low heat until smooth. Meanwhile, in a separate small saucepan, make a roux by melting 4 tablespoons butter and stirring in flour until smooth. Continue to stir and cook over low heat for 10 minutes. Add roux to cheese mixture, mix well and continue cooking for 10 minutes. Add lemon juice, basil, Asiago, salt and pepper (to taste). Let cool. Put mixture in a pastry bag with a star tip and pipe into mushroom caps. Bake at 350 degrees for approximately 12 minutes or until lightly browned. Garnish with garlic butter and chopped chives or parsley.
Serves 6.

1 tsp. butter
1 tsp. garlic
1 oz. white wine
12 oz. natural cream cheese
5 oz. sour cream
4 oz. mushrooms, chopped fine (use stems)
4 Tbsp. butter
1/4 cup flour
1 tsp. lemon juice
1 tsp. fresh basil, chopped
1/2 cup grated Asiago cheese
Salt & pepper to taste
24 large mushroom caps

PROSCIUTTO WILD MUSHROOM BREAD
Kenwood Vineyards

1/4 pound prosciutto, thick slices, diced

3/4 cup Kenwood Vineyards Sauvignon Blanc

8 oz. shallots, peeled and chopped

2 cloves garlic, minced

6 Tbsp. sweet butter

1 cup Italian parsley, chopped

2 pounds mushrooms, a combination of shiitake, chanterelle and oyster, cleaned and sliced

3 Tbsp. fresh thyme, chopped

Salt and pepper to taste

1 large loaf sourdough French bread

Olive Oil

Preheat oven to 350 degrees. In a small sauté pan, cook the prosciutto in 2 tablespoons butter until crisp. Deglaze the pan with the Sauvignon Blanc and set aside.

In a large sauté pan, sauté the onion and garlic in 4 tablespoons butter until transparent, approximately 15 minutes over low heat. Add the mushrooms, parsley, thyme, salt and pepper. Cook until the mushrooms have released their liquid and the mixture is almost dry. Add the prosciutto and Sauvignon Blanc. Cook over medium heat until the wine is reduced to 2 tablespoons. Set aside to cool. Slice the bread in half lengthwise and remove the soft interior, leaving 1/2 inch thickness of bread on the crust surface. Fill the loaf with the prosciutto and mushroom mixture. Replace the top of the loaf and brush the crust with olive oil. Place on a cooking sheet and bake for 20 minutes.

May be served hot or at room temperature. Slice just before serving.

BAKED CHEESE & SUN-DRIED TOMATO ROUNDS
Sonoma Cheese Factory

Cut bread in thin slices and toast lightly on both sides in 350 degree oven. Mix cheese and sun-dried tomatoes and spread thickly on each slice and bake in oven until cheese melts. Garnish with parsley and serve immediately.

1 flute loaf French bread (baguette)

1/2 cup minced sun-dried tomatoes (drained)

2 cups Sonoma Jack cheese

Chopped parsley for garnish

SMOKED SALMON CHEESECAKE
The Tides

Add all crust ingredients together and press firmly onto sides and bottom of a buttered 10-inch springform pan. Refrigerate.

For filling, mix cream, cheese, and salt, using a mixer with paddle attachment. Add eggs, one at a time, only until mixed in. Gently stir in the salmon. Pour filling into the prepared crust. Bake at 325 degrees for 1 hour or until set. Should be served with sour cream and a little salmon roe.

4 oz. melted butter

3 cups French bread crumbs

1 cup grated Gruyere

2 tsp. dried dill

3 1/2 pounds cream cheese

1 cup grated Gruyere

1 tsp. salt

2/3 cup heavy cream

8 eggs

1 lb. smoked salmon, coarsely chopped

Sparkling Wines and a Vista Terrace

Open Daily 10:30 a.m. to 5:30 p.m.
Tours hourly from 11:00 a.m. to 4:00 p.m.

Gloria Ferrer Champagne Caves
23555 Hwy. 121 • Sonoma, CA 95476 • 996-7256

MUSHROOMS IN GARLIC SAUCE
Gloria Ferrer Champagne Caves

6 Tbsp. butter, room temperature

1 Tbsp. minced garlic

1 1/2 lbs. mushrooms, cleaned, stemmed

1 1/2 cup Gloria Ferrer Brut sparkling wine

Salt and pepper to taste

1 to 2 Tbsp. minced fresh parsley or fresh herbs

In 10" skillet, melt 3 tablespoons of the butter over medium heat; add garlic. Cook and stir garlic until lightly browned; add mushrooms. Cook, stirring occasionally, until lightly browned, about 5 minutes. Add Gloria Ferrer Brut; bring to boil. Reduce heat, simmer until liquid is reduced to 1/3 cup, about 10 minutes. Taste and adjust seasoning with salt and pepper. Remove from heat; whisk in remaining butter, bit by bit until sauce is slightly thickened. Arrange mushrooms in serving dish with toothpick inserted in each. Pour sauce over mushrooms; garnish with minced parsley or fresh herbs.

ROMESCO
Gloria Ferrer Champagne Caves

Soak bread in vinegar until soft. Toast almonds in preheated oven for 15 minutes. Grind almonds in food processor. Add bread and process with almonds until a ball forms. Add tomatoes to bread mixture and process until fully combined. Repeat previous step with red bell peppers. Add paprika and salt to mixture and process until spices are incorporated. While processor is on, add olive oil in a slow steady stream until desired consistency is achieved.

Serve Romesco with grilled meats, vegetables, or fish. This sauce is also a wonderful dip for fresh vegetables or bread.

4-6 slices white sandwich bread

4 oz. red wine vinegar

4-6 oz. toasted slivered almonds

4 medium ripe tomatoes (cut into 6ths or 8ths)

2 tsp. Spanish paprika

2 medium red bell pepper (cleaned, seeded and cut into 2" pieces)

1/2 tsp. salt

1/2 cup olive oil

ALI-OLI
Gloria Ferrer Champagne Caves

Combine vegetable oil and olive oil, and set aside.

In blender or food processor (using metal blade) add minced garlic, eggs and Dijon mustard. With machine running, add about half the oil mixture in slow steady stream. Add lemon juice. Add remaining oil. Consistency of ali-oli should be thick and semi-glossy when all oil has been used. Add salt to taste. Run machine for approximately 10 seconds. Transfer ali-oli to bowl, cover and refrigerate.

2 Tbsp. minced garlic

2 eggs

1 1/2 cups vegetable oil

1/2 cup olive oil

2 Tbsp. lemon juice

1/2 Tbsp. Dijon mustard

Salt to taste

MAPLE-BACON PANCAKES
Fensalden Inn

2 cups Bisquick
2 cups shredded Cheddar cheese
1 cup milk
1/2 cup maple syrup
3 Tbsp. sugar
3 eggs
12 slices bacon

Crisp and crumble bacon. Set aside. "Pam" two 9" pie plates. Beat first 6 ingredients with whisk until only small lumps remain. Pour into pans. Bake until pick inserted in center comes out clean, 10-15 minutes. Sprinkle with bacon and remaining cheese. Bake until cheese melts, 3-5 minutes longer. Serve with extra syrup. Serves 10.

fensalden inn

'Land of the Mist and the Sea'

On twenty acres of the Mendocino Coast, Fensalden Inn has a panoramic view of the ocean, Cypress trees and deer feeding in the meadow. The Inn has eight guest quarters, each with private bath; some have fireplaces and ocean views. Breakfast and evening hors d'oeuvres hour make opportunities for much pleasant conversation. Come; relax and enjoy.

Your hosts, Scott and Frances Brazil

p.o. box 99 • albion • ca • 95410 • (707) 937-4042 • 1-800-959-3850

7 miles south of Mendocino on Navarro Ridge Road off Highway 1

No thing more excellent nor more valuable than wine was ever granted mankind by God.

Plato (429–347 B.C.)

BREAKFAST & BRUNCH

ORANGE MARMALADE MUFFINS
Fensalden Inn

2 cups flour
2 1/2 tsp. baking powder
1/3 cup sugar
3/4 tsp. salt
1/3 cup salad oil
One 6 oz. can frozen orange juice concentrate, thawed
1 egg
1/2 cup sweet orange marmalade
1/2 cup chopped nuts

Preheat oven to 400 degrees.

Combine first four ingredients. Mix oil, juice concentrate, and egg. Add all at once to dry mixture. Stir until all is moist. Fold in marmalade and nuts.

Grease regular or gem muffin pans. Fill each cup 2/3 full with batter. Sprinkle sugar over each unbaked muffin, if desired.

Bake 20-25 minutes for regular size-muffins or 12-15 minutes for gem-size. Let cool 5 minutes before removing.

Makes 12 regular muffins or 24 gem-size muffins.

I think it is a great error to consider a heavy tax on wines as a tax on luxury. On the contrary, it is a tax on the health of our citizens.

Thomas Jefferson (1743–1826)

ZUCCHINI BREAD
Frances Brazil, Fensalden Inn

Beat eggs until foamy. Mix in oil, sugar, and vanilla. Add all other ingredients to egg mixture and mix well.

Place in "Pammed" vessels of your choice. Makes 6 small loaves, 1 large loaf or 12 large muffins.

Bake at 325 degrees 1 hour for large loaf.

3 eggs
1 cup oil
2 cups sugar
1 tsp. vanilla
1/2 tsp. nutmeg
1 tsp. salt
1 tsp. soda
1/2 tsp. baking powder
1 1/2 tsp. cinnamon
3 cups flour
2 cups peeled, grated zucchini
3/4 cup nuts

CRAB CREPE FILLING
Fensalden Inn

Prepare basic crepe recipe.

Mix all ingredients together and blend well. Place 2 tablespoons filling on each crepe. Roll up and place, seam down, in baking pan large enough to hold crepes without crowding, but close together.

At this point crepes may be covered and placed in refrigerator overnight or, tightly covered, frozen.

Remove crepes from refrigerator or freezer (thaw briefly) and bake at 350 degrees for 30 minutes, covered, until "bubbly" hot. Serves 20.

1 can (6-oz.) crab meat
8 oz. cream cheese, softened
1/2 cup light sour cream
1/2 tsp. dill weed, crushed
1/4 tsp. tarragon
Dash pepper
1 Tbsp. lemon juice

SPINACH POTATO PIE
Fensalden Inn

4 eggs, beaten
1 Tbsp. milk
1/2 tsp. garlic salt
1/8 tsp. pepper
1/2 tsp. dry mustard
1 1/2 cups O'Brien potatoes
10 oz. package frozen chopped spinach
2 oz. Swiss cheese, shredded

SAUCE:
1/4 cup sour cream
1/4 cup mayonnaise
1 tsp. lemon juice
1/2 tsp. prepared mustard

Combine first 5 ingredients. Add rest of ingredients to egg mix. Pour into "Pammed" 9" pie plate. Bake in preheated 375 degree oven for 40 minutes or until center is done. Remove from oven and let stand five minutes before cutting into 6 portions.

Combine sauce ingredients in small sauce pan over low heat, stirring until hot. Do not boil. Serves 6.

SALSA-CHEESE OMELET
Fensalden Inn

1/2 cup salsa
1 cup shredded Jack cheese
1 cup shredded Cheddar cheese
6 eggs
8 oz. sour cream

Pour salsa in bottom of 10" quiche pan or pie plate. Sprinkle cheeses over salsa. In blender container place eggs; blend until smooth. Pour egg mix over cheese. Bake in 350 degree oven 30-40 minutes or until knife inserted comes out clean.

EGGS FLORENTINE
Whitegate Inn

Squeeze all the liquid out of defrosted spinach. Process cream cheese, spinach, salt, and pepper in food processor until well blended. Divide among 12 4-ounce ramekins, shaping up sides and across bottom. Place mushrooms at the bottom of each hollow in spinach. Place one raw egg in each ramekin and cover with Jack cheese. Place in oven at 375 degrees for 20 minutes. Note: These will continue to cook when removed from the oven.

3 10-oz. packages chopped frozen spinach

1 8-oz. package cream cheese

Salt and pepper (to taste)

1 4-oz. can mushrooms, stems and pieces

12 large eggs

6 oz. grated Jalapeno Jack cheese

HUEVOS WHITEGATE
Whitegate Inn

Using 12 ramekins, line each with small amount of refried beans. Place a teaspoon of salsa on bottom and shake around to spread. Add a light dusting of Cheddar cheese. Put one raw egg, scrambled, in each ramekin and top with a covering of cheese. Bake in preheated 375 degree oven for 20 minutes. Garnish with a teaspoon of sour cream mixed with dill.

1 can vegetarian refried beans

Salsa

Cheddar cheese, shredded

1 dozen eggs

Sour cream

Dill

Sandpiper House Inn

The Sandpiper House was built in 1916 on the rugged cliffs of the Mendocino Coast in the seaside country village of Elk. A perennial garden surrounds the Inn; upon entering, you are warmed by the beauty of redwood and the skilled craftsmanship of the era.

The Inn offers a spectacular ocean front setting overlooking a cove studded with huge sea rocks. The garden path disappears over the bluff to a rare private beach below.

You will enjoy accomodations furnished with antiques and down comforters to cuddle you on misty nights. The morning offers a generous full breakfast; afternoons, tea and homemade baked goods.
In the evenings, guests enjoy complimentary sherry by the living rooms fireplace.

This is truly a place where people can come to refresh, renew their spirit and enjoy the romance of the sea.

Claire and Richard Melrose
Innkeepers

A Seaside Country Inn

5520 So. Highway 1, P.O. Box 49, Elk California 95432 (707) 877-3587

GOLDEN ORANGE PANCAKES
Sandpiper House Inn

1 egg
1 cup light cream
1/4 cup frozen orange juice concentrate
1 cup packaged pancake mix
1/2 cup butter
1 cup sugar
1/2 cup frozen juice concentrate

Combine beaten egg, light cream, and frozen orange juice concentrate. add packaged pancake mix, stir to remove most of the lumps. Bake on greased griddle. Serve with Warm Orange Sauce:

Combine butter, sugar, frozen orange juice concentrate. Bring just to boil, stirring occasionally. Serve warm over pancakes. Serves 4 to 6.

Filling for Golden Orange Pancakes
Sandpiper House Inn

Peel bananas and slice at an angle about 1/2" thick. In sauté pan over medium heat, melt butter or margarine. add brown sugar and swirl until dissolved. Then add rum and bananas. Cook for about 2 minutes, tossing in pan until soft but not mushy. Place inside pancake, roll up and top with warm orange sauce or maple syrup. Top with a dollop of whipped cream or creme fraiche.

4 bananas, ripe but firm
2 Tbsp. unsalted butter or margarine
4 Tbsp. dark brown sugar
1/2 cup dark rum

LEMON PANCAKES
Sandpiper House Inn

Separate eggs and beat egg whites until stiff. Stir together egg yolks, flour, cottage cheese, butter, sugar, salt and lemon zest until well mixed. Fold the egg whites into the egg mixture until there are no yellow or white streaks. Heat electric skillet to 325 degrees, grease lightly and spoon on batter for each cake. Cook slowly about 1 1/2 minutes, then turn and cook about 30 seconds more.

Serve with fresh raspberries and raspberry sauce.

To make raspberry sauce, mix equal parts of raspberry preserves and unsweetened apple juice.

3 eggs, separated
1/2 cup all purpose flour
3/4 cup cottage cheese
1/4 cup butter, melted
2 Tbsp. sugar
1/4 tsp. salt
1/4 tsp. baking powder
1 Tbsp. grated lemon zest

HEAVENLY PUMPKIN GEMS
Sandpiper House Inn

2 cups all purpose flour
1 Tbsp. baking powder
1 tsp. cinnamon
1/4 tsp. nutmeg
1/4 tsp. ginger
1/4 tsp. salt
1/2 cup salad oil or 1/4 pound butter or margarine at room temperature
1/2 cup plus 2 Tbsp. sugar
2 large eggs
1 cup canned pumpkin
1/2 cup sour cream
2 small packages cream cheese, each cut into 6 cubes
3 Tbsp. apricot preserves
1/4 cup sliced almonds

In a large bowl, mix together the first six ingredients. In another bowl, beat oil and 1/2 cup of sugar until blended. Add eggs, pumpkin, and sour cream; beat until thoroughly mixed.

Stir pumpkin mixture into dry ingredients just until moistened. (Butter will be stiff.)

Fill paper-lined muffin tins halfway. Place 1 cheese cube in the center of each cup; top cubes with preserves. Completely cover cheese and jam with remaining batter. Sprinkle tops of muffins with almonds and remaining sugar.

Bake in a 400 degree oven until well browned, about 45 minutes. Remove from pan and cool at least 10 minutes before serving.

PUFFY FRUIT OMELET
Sandpiper House

Preheat oven to 450 degrees. Whisk together egg yolks, flour, baking powder, salt and 3 tablespoons milk until well blended. Whisk in remaining milk. In another bowl, beat egg whites with 3 teaspoons sugar until soft peaks form. Stir half the whites into the yolk mixture, then gently fold in the remaining whites just until blended; do not overmix. Set aside.

Heat oil in large skillet; add apple, pear, 2 teaspoons sugar, lemon juice and cinnamon. Sauté until fruit is tender. Transfer to a non-stick 9" pan, then pour egg mixture on top of fruit. Bake for 10-15 minutes until top is golden brown. Serves 4. Top with Raspberry Sauce.

For Raspberry Sauce, mix equal parts of raspberry jam and unsweetened apple juice. Drizzle each slice before serving.

2 eggs, separated, plus 2 egg whites
2 Tbsp. unbleached all-purpose flour
$1/2$ tsp. baking powder
$1/8$ tsp. salt
$1/2$ cup low fat milk
5 tsp. sugar
1 tsp. safflower oil
1 sweet red apple, cored & cut into $1/2$" pieces
1 pear, preferably Bosc, cored & cut into $1/2$" pieces
1 tsp. fresh lemon juice
$1/4$ tsp. ground cinnamon

FRITTATA ALL VERDURA
Michael Ghilarducci Depot 1870 Restaurant

3 Tbsp. extra-virgin olive oil
1/2 lb. diced zucchini
6 oz. sliced fresh mushrooms
2 bell peppers, seeded and diced
1/2 lb. fresh spinach, blanched & chopped
Salt and pepper to taste
6 eggs, beaten
4 oz. Sonoma Jack cheese, grated

Heat oil in 14" skillet over high heat. Sauté the first three vegetables until cooked, but still firm. Add the spinach and sauté to warm through. Add salt, pepper, and beaten eggs. Stir and cook mixture over medium heat until firm enough to loosen from the pan and flip over. After turning, top with the grated cheese. Cook 2-3 minutes more, until center is done, but still slightly soft. Cut into six wedges and serve at once. Serves 6.

OLE'S SWEDISH HOTCAKES
Little River Inn

MIX TOGETHER:
1 cup flour
1 tsp. sugar
1/4 tsp. salt
1 tsp. baking powder

ADD:
1 1/2 cup milk &
1/2 cup half and half
3 eggs

Separate whites from yokes and beat whites until stiff. Beat yolks. Add yolks to batter, then fold in whites of eggs. Add 3/4 cube of melted butter.

OVERNIGHT SOUR DOUGH BREAD FRENCH TOAST
Frampton House Bed & Breakfast

Spray or grease large baking pan. Cut bread into 1 1/4 inch slices and place in pan. Blend eggs, milk, sugar and spices in blender, or by hand, and pour over bread. Pour melted butter over bread. Cover pan and refrigerate up to 24 hours. Remove from refrigerator, and uncover, in early morning to warm up. Bake at 375 degrees, on low shelf of oven for 30 minutes. Move to higher shelf for 10-15 minutes to brown.

Serve with seasonal fresh fruit, honey, syrup and powdered sugar. Serves 4.

Large loaf sourdough French bread
4 eggs
2 cups milk
1 tsp. sugar
1/2 tsp. each of salt, cinnamon, and nutmeg
1/2 cup butter, melted

COFFEE CAN BREAD
Parducci Winery

Batter will be very sticky.

Combine yeast and warm water. Add rest of ingredients in 5 minutes. Oil a 2-pound coffee can. Place bread dough in can. Oil top. Put top on coffee can. When top pops off, place can in 350 degree oven. Bake 60 minutes. If using 1 pound cans, 45 minutes. Let rest 10 minutes. Open opposite end and push out bread.

1 pkg. yeast
1/2 cup warm water
1/4 tsp. ginger
3 Tbsp. sugar
1 large can evaporated milk
1 tsp. salt
2 Tbsp. oil
4 1/2 cups bread flour

WHOLE WHEAT SCONES
Lisa Hemenway's

3 cups whole wheat flour
12 Tbsp. sweet butter
3/4 cup sugar
2 Tbsp. baking powder
1/2 tsp. baking soda
2 Tbsp. orange zest
1 cup currants
1 cup buttermilk

GLAZE:
3 Tbsp. cream
1/2 cup sugar
1/2 tsp. cinnamon

Blend flour, sugar, baking powder, and baking soda together. Cut in butter, then add orange zest and currants. Add buttermilk and mix just until blended. Boil glaze to dissolve sugar. Cut scones into triangles and glaze. Bake in hot oven at 400 degrees for 20 minutes. Serves 12.

POPPY SEED TEA CAKE
Highland Dell Inn

1/2 pound softened butter
1 cup sugar
4 egg yolks
1/4 cup poppy seeds
2 cups flour
1 tsp. baking soda
1 cup sour cream
4 egg whites, stiffly beaten
1 tsp. cinnamon

Preheat oven to 350 degrees. Butter a tube pan and lightly dust with flour.

Cream together butter, sugar, egg yolks and poppy seeds. Sift together flour and baking soda. Add flour mixture and sour cream alternately to creamed mixture, beginning and ending with flour mixture. Combine egg whites, almond extract, and cinnamon, and fold into batter.

Pour into tube pan. Bake for one hour or until cake tester comes out clean. Cool on cake rack. Serves 8-10.

JOHN DOUGHERTY HOUSE SCONES

Mix flour and baking powder in a bowl. In a large "old stoneware bowl" beat butter until creamy. Add sugar and beat until pale and fluffy. Add eggs, one at a time, beating after each. Add flour mixture; mix only until blended. Add buttermilk; mix only until blended. Sprinkle raisins over batter and fold in.

Using large ice cream scoop, place mounds of dough on ungreased cookie sheet about 2 inches apart. Bake at 350 degrees for about 15 minutes; turn oven to 325 degrees for another 15 minutes. Cool on a wire rack.

3 cups unbleached white flour
1 Tbsp. baking powder
1/2 pound unsalted butter at room temperature
1/4 + 2 Tbsp. white sugar
3 large farm eggs
1/3 cup buttermilk
1/2 cup golden raisins (sultanas)

PEACH CREAM CHEESE CREPES
Pudding Creek Inn

Egg Crepes: In blender combine 3 eggs, 1/2 cup milk, 1/2 cup water, 3/4 cup all-purpose flour, 1 teaspoon sugar, and 1/2 teaspoon salt. Mix until smooth. Bake in 8 inch crepe pan.

Preparation: Peel and slice the peaches to make 2 cups, set aside. In separate bowl, beat cream cheese, sour cream, and whipping cream until smooth. Add the brown sugar and nutmeg. Set aside. Spoon about 1/3 cup of the filling with 3 or 4 peach slices into the center of each crepe. Roll up or fold each crepe into quarters. Place on serving platter, dust with powdered sugar if desired. Serve with whipped cream to spoon over each serving.

2 large peaches
1 package (8 oz.) cream cheese
1/4 cup sour cream
2 Tbsp. whipping cream
5 Tbsp. brown sugar
3/4 tsp. nutmeg
8 crepes (see recipe)

"The rooms here are the most impressive I've seen anywhere ...*four kisses.*"
Best Places to Kiss in N. Calif.

"One of the most luxurious bed and breakfast inns in Napa Valley."
Wine Spectator Magazine

"The best (Napa B&Bs) include Oak Knoll Inn...set in the middle of 600 acres of chardonnay vines complete with hot tub, swimming pool, vast rooms."
The London Times

OAK KNOLL INN

(707) 255-2200

2200 East Oak Knoll Avenue
Napa Valley, CA 94558

STUFFED BAKED PEARS
Oak Knoll Inn

4 ripe pears
Lemon juice

FILLING:
1/2 cup plump raisins
1/4 cup sugar
2 Tbsp. butter
2 tsp. cinnamon
2 Tbsp. cognac (preferably Carneros Alambic)
1/2 tsp. freshly grated nutmeg

Peel pears, cut in half, core, and cut a thin slice off the back so they will sit flat on a plate. Rub with lemon juice so they won't turn brown.

Chop the filling ingredients until finely mixed in a food processor or blender.

Butter a glass baking dish. Stuff pears generously and place them close together in the dish. Cover loosely and bake 1/2 hour at 400 degrees.

Arrange each warm pear half on a pool of vanilla sauce and garnish with a mint sprig at the stem end. A dollop of pear sorbet (optional) on top makes a nice contrast to the warm pear.

For the Vanilla Sauce, whisk ingredients over low heat until slightly thickened.

VANILLA SAUCE:

2 cups half and half

2 tsp. vanilla

1 tsp. Carneros Alambic cognac

2 egg yolks

1/4 cup sugar

2 Tbsp. cornstarch

CLASSIC CREAM SCONES
The Farmhouse Inn

Preheat oven to 425 degrees. Scones take 13-15 minutes to bake. Place all dry ingredients into a large bowl; cut in butter with pastry cutter. Mix in egg, cream, and vanilla.

Mix thoroughly, kneading for about 5 minutes. Batter will be lumpy, thick, and creamy.

Pour onto pastry board spread with the 1 cup flour. Hand mix and hand roll/pat batter to about 1 1/2 inches thick.

Use a biscuit cutter; scones should be about 3 inches in diameter.

Optional glaze: beaten egg with 2 tablespoons water.

Serve right out of the oven. Scones do not keep well and should be made fresh just before serving.

2 cups sifted self-rising flour plus 1 cup for mixing and dusting

1/4 cup sugar

2 Tbsp. baking powder

1 tsp. vanilla

8 Tbsp. sweet butter

2/3 cup heavy cream

1/2 tsp. salt

1 egg

1 cup currants

NAME THAT MUFFIN
Margaret Fox, Cafe Beaujolais

2 cups unsifted white flour
3/4 tsp. salt
3/4 tsp. baking soda
1/4 tsp. baking powder
2 eggs
3/4 cup brown sugar
3/4 cup corn oil
3/4 tsp. vanilla extract
1 1/3 cups prepared fruit or vegetables
1 1/2 tsp. cinnamon
1 1/2 tsp. ground ginger
1/3 cup poppy seeds
3/4 cup coarsely chopped toasted walnuts

The personality of this muffin changes depending on the fruit or vegetable that is added to the batter. Ms. Fox has used leftovers or bruised but still edible fruits or vegetables. She has used apples, pears, oranges, zucchini, tomatoes, plums, even fresh pumpkin. An interesting option is to divide the batter into several batches and add different fruits or vegetables to each batch.

Preheat oven to 400 degrees. Sift together the flour, salt, baking soda, and baking powder. In a separate bowl, whip the eggs with the sugar and oil. Stir in the vanilla, whatever fruits or vegetables you are using, the spices, and the poppy seeds. Add the flour mixture and the nuts. Do not overmix.

Spoon the batter into greased or papered muffin cups, filling each about three-quarters full. Bake for 25-30 minutes until golden brown. Makes about 18 muffins.

HUEVOS RANCHEROS
Margaret Fox, Cafe Beaujolais

If this dish is prepared for more than one person, increase salsa by about 1/4 cup per additional serving.

Heat salsa in a small frying pan.

Beat each egg into a separate small bowl and when salsa is hot (boiling), gently add eggs to sauce. Turn down heat to low. Cover pan. Cook eggs for about 3 minutes, occasionally spooning sauce over eggs and also checking to see that egg hasn't stuck to bottom of pan. Heat tortilla(s), either in a skillet on top of the stove or in a 350 degree oven. Sprinkle cheese evenly over the surface of the tortilla(s) and let melt. Remove from oven and spread with chili. If using lettuce, place around edge of tortilla(s). With a large spoon, carefully remove eggs from salsa and place in middle of your creation. Spoon salsa over top, garnish with olives, sour cream, and cilantro. Serve immediately.

PER SERVING:

1 cup salsa

2 eggs

1/4–1/2 cup grated Jack or Cheddar cheese

2 corn tortillas or 1 large flour tortilla (10-12 inches wide)

About 3/4 cup Black Bean Chili, heated

About 1/2 cup shredded crunchy lettuce (optional)

1 Tbsp. chopped black olives

Sour cream

Chopped cilantro

CARAMELIZED APPLESAUCE
Margaret Fox, Cafe Beaujolais

About 4 1/2 lbs. cooking apples (Granny Smith)

1 1/3 cups water

Juice from half a lemon

2 cups sugar

1/2 vanilla bean, split in half lengthwise

Peel and core the apples and place peels and cores in a saucepan. Add water, bring to a boil, lower the heat and simmer for 5 minutes. Cut each apple into 6 wedges, place in a bowl and toss with lemon juice, trying to coat each surface of every wedge.

Strain the cooking liquid from the peels and cores through a sieve over a large pan, pressing hard to extract as much liquid as possible. Add sugar to the liquid in the pan and bring slowly to a boil, stirring gently with a wooden spoon until the sugar melts. If any sugar sticks to the sides of the pan, clean it off with a moistened pastry brush.

When the syrup comes to a boil, raise the heat and boil rapidly for about 10 minutes, until it reaches 313 degrees, stirring occasionally. As soon as the syrup begins to turn a caramel color, add the apples and the vanilla beans. Be very careful not to get any of this syrup on you. It is incredibly hot. If you do, immerse the burned area in cold water immediately.

Cook for 5 minutes, then lower the heat, cook at a slow boil for about 20 minutes, or until the apples begin to fall apart. The finished sauce should be chunky, not smooth. Don't stir the apples, shake the pan gently.

GERMAN PANCAKES
Highland Dell Inn

Preheat oven to 375 degrees.
Beat eggs until fluffy. Add sugar and milk slowly to the egg mixture. Add the flour, salt, and vanilla. Beat until smooth. Butter a 12" skillet with a heatproof handle with a thick layer of butter.
Pour batter and bake for 40-45 minutes or until light brown and puffed up.
Remove and sprinkle with powdered sugar, serve hot with lots of butter and warm syrup.
Serves 6.

4 eggs
$1/3$ cup sugar
2 cups whole milk
$2^{1}/_{4}$ cups flour
1 tsp. salt
2 tsp. vanilla
Powdered sugar

SPICED APPLE CIDER
Whitegate Inn

Simmer 15 minutes. Serve hot with fresh orange slices studded with cloves.
10 servings.

2 quarts apple cider
1 tsp. allspice
1 tsp. cinnamon
2 sticks cinnamon
Few whole cloves

SOUTH OF THE BORDER FRITTATA
The Inn on Cedar Street

16 oz. turkey sausage (preferably hot sausage)
6 eggs
1 cup cream
1 1/2 tsp. baking powder
1/2 tsp. salt
2 Tbsp. flour
6 slices white bread, decrusted and cubed
1 can (14 oz.) diced green chilis
1 1/2 lbs. sharp Cheddar cheese, grated
1 Tbsp. butter
Sour cream
Avocado (guacamole)
Hot sauce
6 tomato wedges

Cook sausage until all pink is gone and set aside.

Vigorously whisk the eggs and cream; add baking powder, salt, flour, and bread cubes. Add a dash of pepper, then blend.

Lightly butter a 2 quart glass casserole dish.

Sprinkle half of the sausage into a casserole dish and layer with half of the chilis and then half of the cheese. Repeat layers with remaining sausage, chilis, and cheese.

Pour egg mixture over casserole and dot with butter. Bake at 350 degrees for 40-45 minutes. Let set for 15-20 minutes.

Serve with a scoop of sour cream, guacamole, and a slice of tomato.

Serves 6.

BROCCOLI CHEESE PUFFS
Whitegate Inn

Mix all ingredients together except Parmesan cheese. Place in 1/2 ramekins, greased with margarine. Cook at 350 degrees for 30 minutes until puffed. Top with Parmesan cheese.

1/2 package frozen chopped broccoli, defrosted

1 small can mushrooms, stems & pieces

1 small container Ricotta cheese

4 oz. shredded Mozzarella cheese

4 oz. Pepper Jack cheese

10 eggs

2 tsp. Spice Island salad herbs

1/2 tsp. seasoned salt

Shredded Parmesan

MARGARETT PARDUCCI'S ZUCCHINI PANCAKES
Parducci Winery

Mix ingredients in order. Fry in vegetable oil and drain.

2 cups grated or chopped zucchini

3 Tbsp. chopped fresh parsley (1 1/2 Tbsp. dried)

1 clove garlic, minced (1/8 tsp. garlic powder)

1 egg

1 cup commercial biscuit mix

Salt & pepper to taste

HOT APPLE OATMEAL CEREAL
Whale Watch Inn

4 cups milk
1/2 cup brown sugar
2 Tbsp. butter
1/2 tsp. salt
1 Tbsp. cinnamon
2 cups old-fashioned oats
2 cups chopped apples (green and tart)
1 cup raisins
1 cup chopped nuts
Vanilla, optional

Preheat oven to 350 degrees. Bring milk, sugar, butter, salt, and cinnamon to a boil in a heavy pot. Add the remaining ingredients and bake, uncovered, for 30-35 minutes in buttered casserole.

Serves 6-8.

One of the top ten Bed and Breakfast Inns in California
- San Francisco Focus Magazine

The Whale Watch Inn

on California's Mendocino Coast defines matchless luxury. It is privacy, personal service, scenic beauty, 18 unique rooms & hideaway suites, ocean views, fine linens, down comforters, fireplaces, two-person whirlpool baths, breakfast in bed, and "banana belt" weather.

Owners: Jim and Kazuko Popplewell ■ Reservations (800) WHALE-42
35100 Highway 1, Gualala, CA 95445

SPINACH-MUSHROOM FETA FILLOS
Whale Watch Inn

Sauté mushrooms, onion, and garlic in olive oil. Remove from heat. Add feta cheese, basil leaves, and spinach. Mix well and let set to "bloom" overnight for better flavor. If in a hurry let set for one hour.

Carefully read instructions on fillo dough package. Take one full sheet, brush inside with butter, and fold 1/3 into center. Fold other side in 1/3, slightly overlapping first 1/3, again butter inside with butter. You now have a long narrow strip of fillo dough. Fold a generous tablespoon of filling onto fillo leaf. Brush with melted butter on top of folds and fold into a triangle shape (similar to military flag folding). On last fold, brush with melted butter and sprinkle poppyseeds with butter for garnish. Can be frozen for later use, or bake immediately on an ungreased baking sheet in a 350 degree oven for 15-20 minutes or until golden brown.

1 lb. mushrooms
1 large chopped onion
4 cloves garlic, chopped
1/4 cup olive oil
1 lb. Feta cheese, crumbled
1 bunch fresh chopped basil leaves
1 lb. chopped frozen spinach (squeeze out excess liquid)
1 lb. package fillo dough leaves (if frozen, thaw)
Poppy seeds for garnish (optional)

BREAD PUDDING WITH WHISKEY SAUCE
Carol Hall, Hot Pepper Jelly Company

10 slices day-old bread, broken into small pieces
4 cups milk, scalded
1 cup cream
4 eggs
1 cup sugar
1/4 cup butter, melted
Juice and zest of 1 lemon
1 tsp. vanilla
1 tsp. cinnamon
1/2 tsp. nutmeg
1/2 cup golden raisins

VANILLA WHISKEY SAUCE:
3 egg yolks
1 cup sugar
1 tsp. vanilla
1 1/2 cups milk
1 Tbsp. cornstarch
1/4 cup water
1 1/2 ozs. brandy

Combine bread, milk, and cream. Beat eggs, add sugar, and mix well. Stir in bread mixture, vanilla and spices. Add and mix in butter and raisins. Pour into buttered 2 quart baking dish. Bake at 350 degrees for about 1 hour or until knife inserted in center comes out clean.

For the sauce, put slightly beaten egg yolks in a saucepan, then add next 3 ingredients and blend well. Cook over medium low heat (stirring constantly) until mixture comes to a boil. Blend cornstarch and water and stir into hot mixture. Continue cooking until thickened. Remove from heat and stir in brandy.

Serve warm over bread pudding.

ZUCCHINI QUICHE
Whitegate Inn

Spread the bottom of a pastry shell with mustard. Bake on cookie sheet in 450 degree oven for 10 minutes. Cool. Reduce oven heat to 350 degrees. Sprinkle one cup of Jack cheese in the bottom of the pastry shell. Layer mushrooms, then zucchini, on top of cheese. Beat together cream cheese, egg yolks, egg, and whipping cream. Carefully pour mixture over cheese. Place on cookie sheet and bake in 350 degree oven for 45 minutes until top is puffed and golden and knife inserted in the middle comes out clean. Let stand 5 minutes before cutting. Serves 6-8.

1 9½" to 10" unbaked pastry shell

2 Tbsp. Dijon mustard

2 cups grated zucchini

1 4-oz. can mushrooms, stems & pieces

2 cups Monterey Jack cheese, grated

1 8-oz. package cream cheese

½ cup whipping cream

2 egg yolks

1 egg

Wine is inspiring and adds greatly to the joy of living.

Napoleon (1769–1821)

Buena Vista
C A R N E R O S

Visit California's Oldest Premium Winery

Award Winning Wines

•

Rare and Current Vintages

•

Guided & Self-Guided Tours

•

Group Tours by Reservation

•

Gift & Gourmet Food Shop

•

Picnic Grounds

•

Art Gallery

•

Weddings

Open Daily 10:30 - 4:30
18000 Old Winery Road
Sonoma, CA (800) 926-1266

SOUPS & SALADS

Drink a glass of wine after your soup and you steal a ruble from the doctor.

Russian Proverb

TOMATO SOUP WITH GRILLED SEA SCALLOPS AND CHERVIL
Fred Halpert, Brava Terrace

6 lbs. fresh tomatoes, or 3 28-oz. cans crushed tomatoes

6 oz. onions, sliced

6 Tbsp. extra virgin olive oil

4 Tbsp. sherry vinegar

2 peeled garlic cloves, sliced

2 Tbsp. tomato paste

1 bunch fresh chervil, or 2 Tbsp. dried

4 Tbsp. aged red wine vinegar

5 Tbsp. water

2 sprigs lemon thyme

$1/2$ tsp. dried, coarsely ground pepper

16 sea scallops

Peel, seed, and chop fresh tomatoes.

Sweat garlic and onions together in 6 tablespoons olive oil. Add the tomato paste and water, simmer, then add tomatoes, chervil, thyme, salt and pepper, and the vinegars. Cook for $1/2$ hour. Run through food processor, then pass through fine strainer. Season to taste.

Char-grill or broil scallops until just barely done. Put 2 in each bowl and top with the hot soup. Garnish with fresh chervil leaves or parsley. Serves 8.

GOLDEN POTATO SOUP
Spring Street Restaurant

Combine broth, potatoes, onion, and carrots in large saucepan. Simmer until potatoes are tender, about 15 minutes. Mash potatoes in liquid for thickening. Stir in remaining ingredients and heat gently.
Serves 6 to 8.

3 cups beef broth (or 3 cups water with 3 Tbsp. beef base)

1 medium onion, diced

$2^1/_2$ cups diced potatoes

3 carrots, grated

3 cups milk

2 Tbsp. chopped parsley

1 cup sour cream

Salt and pepper to taste

VEGETARIAN BLACK BEAN SOUP
Spring Street Restaurant

Rinse and sort beans, discarding any foreign material, and combine with water. Bring to boil for two minutes, then set aside for one hour. Add beer and simmer until beans are tender; add rest of ingredients and simmer until thickened, about 2 to 3 hours. Add more water as needed to maintain proper consistency, and salt and pepper to taste. Garnish each bowl with sour cream and chopped green onions.

2 lbs. dried black beans

8 cups water

1 can of beer

3 onions, diced

4 cloves of garlic, diced

1 bunch of fresh cilantro, chopped

2 cups picante salsa (any good bottled salsa)

Salt and pepper to taste

FRESH ASPARAGUS SOUP
The Restaurant

2 pounds asparagus, chopped
3 medium onions, diced
3/4 pound butter
2 cups cream
4 oz. cooking sherry
4 quarts chicken stock
2 cups flour
Salt, pepper, bay leaves, thyme, rosemary

Bring stock to boil. Sauté 1/2 pound butter, onions, and 1 1/2 cups flour to make a thick paste; add 4 ounces sherry and enough stock to blend. Blend in blender. Make roux with 1/4 pound butter and rest of flour; add roux to remaining stock. Mix with blended soups; add cream.

Heat remaining asparagus in boiling water for 2 minutes, drain and add to soup. Serve. May substitute mushrooms.

CREAMY RED BELL PEPPER SOUP
Chez Cafe & Overnight

4 red bell peppers, seeded and coarsely chopped
1 leek, sliced
2 cloves garlic, coarsely chopped
2 red potatoes, diced
1 tsp. chopped fresh rosemary
4 Tbsp. olive oil
2 cups heavy cream
Salt and black pepper
Sour cream, optional

Sauté red bells in olive oil over high heat until they begin to brown. Add garlic, leeks, rosemary, and potatoes, and toss in hot oil for 2 minutes. Add enough water to cover and simmer until potatoes are very tender.

Cool 5 minutes. Puree in food processor. Return to soup pot. Add cream and salt and pepper to taste. Serve garnished with thinned sour cream if desired.

ROY'S SALMON SALAD
Landmark Vineyards

For the dressing, place all ingredients, except pepper, into food processor or blender and mix well. Pour over salad, toss well, add fresh ground pepper.

Serve with Landmark 1990 Sonoma County Chardonnay.

1 7-oz. can Griffin Greatland smoked salmon, drained

2-3 stalks celery, sliced or chopped

1 tomato, sliced

1 cucumber, quartered and cubed

1 red onion, sliced or coarsely chopped

1 avocado, cubed

1-2 heads Romaine lettuce, torn into small pieces

DRESSING

1/2 to 1/4 cup light olive oil

2 Tbsp. lemon juice

1/4 to 1/3 cup Barengo (or any strong) vinegar

1/8 tsp. fresh dill

1 to 3 cloves garlic, minced

Coarse salt (to taste)

Freshly ground pepper

SIMI

A CENTURY OF STYLE AND INNOVATION

For a glimpse of the past and a tour of the future....
Come and visit the oldest and most modern winery
in the Alexander Valley

- Complimentary tastes of award-winning wines
- Food and wine pairings
- Reserve tasting programs
- Picnic facilities
- Daily tours at 11:00, 1:00 & 3:00

16275 Healdsburg Avenue • Healdsburg, CA 95448
707 / 433-6921 • Open daily 10-4:30

STEAK SALAD WITH BLUE CHEESE DRESSING
Chef Mary Evely, Simi Winery

1-2 lge. onions, thinly sliced
Flour for dredging
Oil for deep frying
Salt and pepper
2 trimmed New York steaks (about 1 1/2 lbs.)
6 large handfuls of salad greens (try arugula and watercress)

BLUE CHEESE DRESSING
1/4 lb. Oregon blue cheese
1 cup light sour cream
2 Tbsp. chopped chives
1 Tbsp. white wine vinegar
Extra chives for garnish

Separate the onions into rings and toss to coat with flour seasoned with a little salt and pepper. Preheat oil to 375 degrees and fry the onion rings in small batches until light brown. Spread on a baking sheet lined with paper towels and salt lightly.

Preheat grill or broiler. Salt and pepper the steaks and grill 5 minutes per side for rare. Set aside to rest for at least 5 minutes. Place dressing ingredients in a food processor and puree.

Divide greens among 4 to 6 dinner plates. Slice steak and arrange slices on the plates with the greens, top with dressing and a handful of the fried onion rings. Garnish with chives. Serves 4-6.

ROASTED PUMPKIN RISOTTO WITH FRESH SAGE
Chef Mary Evely, Simi Winery

Preheat the oven to 350 degrees. Slice off the top 1/2 inch of the pumpkin and scoop out the seeds. Sprinkle salt and pepper into the cavity. Put one tablespoon of cream and one sage leaf in each pumpkin, replace the lid, and bake in a pan until just tender, 30-35 minutes.

When the pumpkins are cool, discard the sage leaves and empty the cream into a medium bowl. Remove the flesh of the pumpkin to the bowl, using a small spoon. Make sure to leave enough flesh in the shell to prevent it from collapsing. Set pumpkins aside.

Heat the chicken stock until it is just simmering. In a heavy bottomed pot, melt the butter and cook the onion over medium heat until transluscent. Add the rice, stirring to coat. Add the Chardonnay and cook until the wine has been absorbed. Then begin adding the hot stock just to cover the rice, keeping liquid bubbling gently. Continue adding stock as it is absorbed into the rice, stirring with each addition.

Return the pumpkin shells to the oven to reheat. Cut the remaining eight sage leaves into chiffonade. Test rice by tasting it. It should be al dente, not hard or mushy, and the sauce should look creamy. You may not need to use the entire amount of stock. Stir in the chiffonade and correct the seasoning. Add in the reserved cream and pumpkin flesh.

Spoon risotto into the pumpkin shells. Prop the pumpkin top against the side, sprinkle with grated cheese and serve immediately, garnished with sage sprigs and radicchio, if desired. Serves 8.

Suggested wine: Simi Chardonnay

8 miniature pumpkins

Salt

Freshly ground white pepper

1/2 cup heavy cream

16 fresh sage leaves

3 Tbsp. unsalted butter

1 medium onion, chopped

1 1/2 cups Arborio rice

1/2 cup Simi Chardonnay

4-5 cups chicken stock

1 cup freshly grated Asiago cheese

OPTIONAL GARNISH

sage sprigs and radicchio leaves

Meadowood
Napa Valley

"A Napa Valley fantasy... the utmost in luxury"

Jacqueline Kileen
San Francisco Focus

- INVITING ACCOMMODATIONS
- INSPIRED CUISINE
- OUTSTANDING CONFERENCE & SPORTS FACILITIES

900 Meadowood Lane • St. Helena, CA 94574
(707) 963-3646 • 800-458-8080

PRAWN SALAD WITH ROAST PEPPERS
Roy Breiman, Chef de Cuisine

12 medium-sized prawns
1 roasted bell pepper
1 fennel bulb (cut in quarters)
6 oz. baby spinach
1 bunch chives (cut in 2" pieces)
5 sprigs parsley
1 shallot (chopped)
4 oz. black nicoise olives (pitted)
6 oz. olive oil
3 oz. Balsamic vinegar

Clean prawns, cut in half, season with salt and pepper and place in refrigerator. Wrap red pepper in aluminum and place in 500 degree oven with a little olive oil and salt for approximately 15-20 minutes. Remove skin and chop in $1/2$" cubes. Place quartered fennel in 3 ounces of olive oil in sauce pan on medium heat, cooking slowly until tender. Approximately 15 minutes.

Combine spinach, parsley, chives, shallots, olives, roasted pepper, fennel, salt and pepper in large mixing bowl. With remaining olive oil, sauté prawns at a high temperature, watching closely not to overcook. Before removing, deglaze the pan with the Balsamic vinegar. Add contents of pan to bowl of herbs and mix thoroughly. Serve immediately.

WARM CALAMARI SERVED IN A WHITE BEAN VINAIGRETTE
Roy Breiman, Chef de Cuisine, The Restaurant at Meadowood

Soak beans in unsalted water 3-4 hours before cooking. Remove excess water. Set aside.

In a sauce pan, combine sliced onion, bacon, thyme, bay leaf. Brown slightly before adding beans and salted water. Cook over medium heat until tender, approximately 3 hours.

Clean calamari by removing the eye and main cartilage, rinsing completely, cut the calamari shell in $1/4$ inch rings. Combine the tentacles. Place in refrigerator.

Remove cooked beans from original pan and place in a sauté pan with a little cooking liquid. Combine shallots, $1/2$ of the chopped chives, $1/2$ chopped tomato, 2 ounces Balsamic vinegar, 1 ounce olive oil. Warm over medium heat. Season with salt and pepper and set aside.

Cook sliced calamari in a sauté pan over high heat with remaining olive oil, garlic, tomato and chives for approximately 1 minute. Remove from flame and begin to dress plate.

When dressing the plate, spoon 6-7 large tablespoons of the white bean mixture onto a serving plate. Place an equal amount of calamari on top of the beans. Serve warm with some fresh sprigs of Italian parsley.

12 pieces fresh calamari

8 oz. Great Northern white beans

3 tomatoes (diced)

6 cloves garlic (chopped fine)

2 bunches chives (chopped)

16 oz. water (salt water with approximately 3 large pinches)

2 oz. Balsamic vinegar

2 oz. olive oil

1 onion (sliced)

3 slices bacon

$1/2$ bunch fresh thyme

2 bay leaves

12 sprigs Italian parsley

AUSTRALIAN PIE FLOATER
Geyser Peak Winery

1 1/2 lbs. ground beef
2 beef stock cubes
Salt and pepper to taste
2 cups water
Pinch of nutmeg
2 Tbsp. plain flour
1 1/4 cups water (extra)
1 tsp. soy sauce

PIE BASE
2 cups plain flour
1/2 tsp. salt
2/3 cup water
2 oz. drippings or margarine

PIE TOP
3 sheets frozen puff pastry
1 egg yolk
1 tsp. water

The recipes that follow will provide 12 pie floaters. Place one heated pie floater in center of soup bowl. Cover with one ladle pea and ham soup. Top with a splash of ketchup (yes, ketchup) to taste.

Brown ground beef over low heat and drain off surplus fat. Add crumbled stock cubes, water, salt, pepper, and nutmeg. Stir until boiling. Reduce heat, cover, simmer gently 20 minutes, then remove from heat. Combine extra water and flour and stir until flour is smooth. Add flour mixture to meat, stir until combined. Return to heat, stir until meat boils and thickens. Add soy sauce for color and stir until combined. Simmer, uncovered, 5 to 10 minutes, then remove from heat and allow to cool.

For pie base, sift flour and salt into bowl. Place water and margarine into saucepan, stir until melted, and remove from heat. Make a well in center of dry ingredients; add liquid and stir until combined. Turn out onto lightly floured surface, knead lightly. Roll out to line 12 greased muffin tins. Cut away excess pastry from side of tins. Fill center with cold meat filling.

Cut puff pastry to fit pies. Wet edges of base and press tops into place. Pierce center with pointed knife. Brush tops with combined egg yolk and water. Bake in hot oven 5-10 minutes. Reduce to moderate heat and bake another 10 minutes.

THICK SPLIT PEA AND HAM SOUP
Geyser Peak Winery

Combine all ingredients in large stock pot, bring to a boil. Simmer gently 2 hours, until thick. Remove bones, cut meat away. Add meat to soup. Season with salt and pepper, adjust thickness with additional water.

2 ham bones

1 onion, finely chopped

1 carrot, grated

1 pkg. (12 oz.) split peas

4 pints water (approximate)

Salt and pepper to taste

No thing more excellent nor more valuable than wine was ever granted mankind by God.

Plato (429–347 B.C.)

SONOMA VALLEY SALAD FOR TWO
Equus Restaurant

12 oz. spring mix (salad)
1 apple, cored, halved and sliced
1/2 basket raspberries
1/2 basket blueberries
4-6 oz. Raspberry Vinaigrette dressing
4 oz. Candied Pecans
4 oz. brie, split in two, floured, egged and bread crumbs, baked until warm inside

Raspberry Vinaigrette

1/2 cup raspberry vinegar
2 Tbsp. Dijon mustard
1 oz. raspberry puree
1 Tbsp. sugar
2 cups oil
(1 cup walnut oil, 1 cup peanut)

Candied Pecans

4 oz. pecans
1/4 cube butter
1/4 cup brown sugar

Salad: Toss all together except cheese. Add at last minute on plate, warm.

Raspberry Vinaigrette: Combine raspberry vinegar, mustard, and raspberry puree, sugar. Drizzle oil into mixture while whisking to emulsify. May be done in blender. Salt and pepper.

Candied Pecans: Place pecans on baking sheet in low oven, 200 degrees, for 25 minutes or until lightly toasted. On the stove melt butter and add brown sugar. Stir until sugar is a light caramel, add pecans to coat, then place on sheet pan to cool.

CHESTNUT SOUP
Inn at Occidental

In stock pot, melt butter, cook vegetables for 20 minutes. Stir in broth and herbs. Add chestnuts and simmer covered for 20 minutes. Puree in blender. Put back in stock pot and add madeira and cream. Simmer.

6 Tbsp. butter
1 cup chopped celery
1 cup chopped carrot
1 cup chopped onion
3/4 pound potatoes, peeled and chopped
3 cups chicken broth
2 1/2 cups beef broth
1/4 cup chopped parsley
1 tsp. thyme
1 tsp. sage
1 tsp. basil
1 15 1/2 ounce chestnuts, drained
1/2 cup madeira
1 cup heavy cream
Salt & pepper

Water separates the people of the world; wine unites them.

Anonymous

WARM SPINACH SALAD WITH SCALLOPS
Kevin Morrissey, Wermuth Winery

1 Tbsp. olive oil

2 thin slices pancetta or bacon, cut into thin slices

1 carrot, cut in thin matchsticks

6 shiitake or button mushrooms, sliced

1 shallot, finely chopped

1/3 lb. scallops

1/2 cup Wermuth Bone Sauvignon Blanc

2-3 leaves of sorrel, thinly sliced, or the juice of 1/2 lemon

2 Tbsp. butter

1/4 tsp. fresh black pepper

3 cups fresh spinach, cleaned, washed and dried

In a pan, heat oil until very hot. Carefully add pancetta and cook briefly. Add carrots and mushrooms and cook until slightly brown. Add shallots and scallops and continue to cook for 60 seconds. Add the Wermuth Bone Vineyard Sauvignon Blanc and cook until scallops are just firm.

Remove scallops and place on the spinach that has previously been arranged on plates. Add the sorrel and butter and cook until butter melts. Add salt and pepper to taste.

Pour liquid with vegetables over the salad and serve. Serves 2.

WARM CHICKEN SAUSAGE AND POTATO SALAD
Joe Harris, Chocolate Moosse

Preheat oven to 500 degrees, Grind spice in coffee mill. Combine all ingredients in food processor and process until mixture feels gummy. Place into pastry bag without tip and pipe long sausage shapes onto cookie sheet. Bake for 15 minutes.

Combine orange juice, tarragon, garlic, salt and pepper in bowl. Whisk in olive oil to make dressing.

Cook potatoes in salted boiling water until tender but not mushy. Combine with other ingredients and dressing while hot so that the flavors penetrate the potatoes.

Slice sausages into bite-sized pieces. Sauté sausages with potato salad until warmed, about 1/2 minute. Serve with green salad. Serves 6.

1 lb. dark chicken meat, with skin on, cut in pieces

1 tsp. salt

1 tsp. dried thyme

1/4 tsp. sage

1/2 tsp. pepper flakes

1 tsp. fennel seeds

1/2 tsp. anise seeds

2 cloves garlic

2 Tbsp. whiskey

1/4 cup ice

1 1/2 lbs. new potatoes, cubed

1/2 medium red onion, diced

2 ribs celery, diced

1/2 red bell pepper, diced

Juice of 1 orange

2 Tbsp. chopped fresh tarragon

1 clove garlic, chopped fine

1/2 cup olive oil

Salt & pepper to taste

EXPERIENCE
INLAND MENDOCINO WINE COUNTRY

and taste the top-quality wines produced in this headwater Region of the Russian River

Parducci
TASTING • TOURS
Open Daily 9-5
Fine California Wines Since 1932

Fetzer VINEYARDS
from the earth to the table
Open daily 9-5

DUNNEWOOD VINEYARDS
OPEN DAILY 10 - 5

JEPSON
Open daily 10 - 5

McDowell
Open 10-5 Daily

Zellerbach
Tasting Daily 10-5

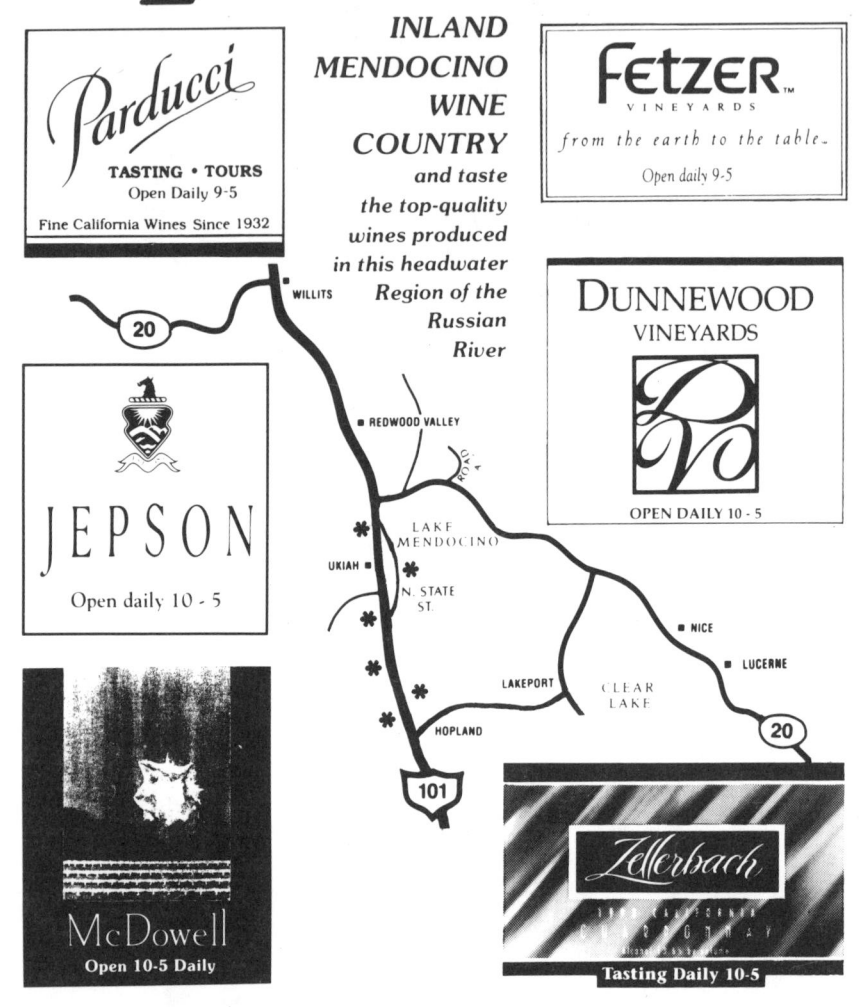

ZELLERBACH WINERY
Between Hopland & Ukiah
2 miles on McNab Ranch Road
707-462-2423

PARDUCCI WINE CELLARS
501 Parducci Road
Ukiah, CA 95482
707-462-WINE

McDOWELL VALLEY VINEYARDS
13441 Hwy. 101
Hopland, CA 95449
707-744-1516

JEPSON VINEYARDS
10400 South Highway 101
Ukiah, CA 95482
707-468-8936

DUNNEWOOD VINEYARDS
2399 North State Street
Ukiah, CA 95482
707-462-2987

FETZER VINEYARDS
P.O. Box 611
Hopland, CA 95449
707-744-1737

ENTREES

There is a considerable body of evidence that lower levels of drinking decreases the risk of death from coronary artery disease.

The National Institute on Alcohol Abuse & Alcoholism

GRILLED OPA WITH ROASTED TOMATO, PECAN VINAIGRETTE
Bistro Ralph

2 lbs. fresh Opa (or substitute swordfish) portioned for 4

2 lbs. vine ripe tomatoes (top quality), peeled, chopped and seeded

2 shallots, chopped

1/2 cup roasted pecans, coarsely chopped

1/4 cup plus 1 Tbsp. virgin olive oil

1/8 cup red wine vinegar

Salt and pepper

Mizuna leaves and caramelized carrots for garnish

Prepare the grill for the Opa. Grill all fish over hot coals so that it sears immediately and retains its juices. Slightly undercook this fish to benefit its full flavor and texture. Use 1 tablespoon of olive oil to coat fish before grilling.

To prepare the tomato-pecan vinaigrette, put the tomatoes and shallots in a baking dish and place in a preheated 500 degree oven for approximately 45 minutes or until almost all the juice has been cooked off.

Using a blender, puree half of the roasted tomato mixture and add 1/4 cup virgin olive oil and the red wine vinegar. In a bowl combine the puree, remaining roasted tomatoes and chopped pecans; adjust acid and season. It is best to let the vinaigrette sit for at least an hour before serving. Season and grill fish, place on mizuna leaves, spoon vinaigrette over the top and serve.

COQUILLE ST. JACQUE
The Wharf, Noyo Fishing Village

Put first seven ingredients in large pot. Bring to a boil, reduce heat and simmer until scallops are lightly cooked. Thicken with roux. Blend in heavy cream and immediately add the egg yolks. Continue to simmer until mixture is set. Turn off heat and add sour cream. Garnish with Parmesan before serving. Serves approximately 6 to 8 main courses.

1/4 lb. butter
3/4 cup Parducci white wine
1 cup mushrooms, sliced
6 scallions, sliced
2-3 lbs. medium scallops, drained
1 Tbsp. salt
1/2 tsp. white pepper

Roux
1/4 lb. butter
1/2 cup flour
1 cup heavy cream
4 egg yolks
1 cup sour cream
Parmesan cheese

Good wine is a good familiar creature if it be well used, exclaim no more against it.

Othello, William Shakespeare (1564—1616)

PRAWNS BORDELAISE
La Gare French Restaurant

8 prawns (under 15 to the pound)
Flour
1 egg (for egg wash)
2 Tbsp. oil
Salt and pepper
1/4 tsp. shallots
1/4 tsp. garlic
2 oz. butter
1/4 tsp. lemon juice
1 tsp. parsley
1 cup white wine

Devein shrimp and butterfly through the back. Dust with flour and dip in egg wash. Heat a skillet with approximately 2 tablespoons oil. When hot (not smoking), lay prawns flat, and brown, then turn prawns and add salt and pepper. Drain oil, add shallots, garlic, butter, and lemon juice. Sauté quickly, then add parsley and white wine and let sauce thicken. If sauce breaks, add a little more wine to bring it back to proper consistency. Serves 2.

PEDRONCELLI

SONOMA COUNTY WINES

FAMILY OWNED AND OPERATED FOR OVER 60 YEARS

•

Visit our tasting room overlooking our Estate Vineyards in Dry Creek Valley.

Tasting and Sales daily, 10 a.m. through 5 p.m.

•

1220 Canyon Rd., Geyserville   707-857-3531

ITALIAN BAKED VEGETABLES
Pedroncelli Winery

With a vegetable peeler, make 1/2 inch wide strips down sides of eggplants. Cut them crosswise into 1/4 inch thick slices. Spread, sliced, on a large platter and sprinkle them with 1/2 teaspoon salt; set aside 15 minutes, then rinse and pat slices dry on paper towels.

Coat bottom of a 10"x15" inch baking dish with 2 tablespoons of oil; set aside. Adjust oven rack to lowest position. Heat oven to 450 degrees.

Thinly slice the potatoes and spread in a layer in the bottom of the baking dish. Sprinkle with salt and pepper. Slice the onions and spread them over the potatoes in an even layer, add salt and pepper. Cut the peppers into 3/8 inch rings and arrange them over the tomatoes. Sprinkle salt and pepper lightly over the vegetables, then drizzle the remaining olive oil and wine over the top.

Cover the dish loosely with aluminum foil. Bake 25 minutes. Lower oven heat to 325 degrees and bake 45 minutes longer or until knife inserted into vegetables meets no resistance.

Uncover and cool. (Can prepare, cool, and set aside, loosely covered, up to 6 hours.) Serve warm or at room temperature.

NOTE: You may add your choice of fresh herbs to each layer if you wish. I suggest summer savory or thyme with the Fume Blanc. Serves 8. You may also use different vegetables.

1 1/4 pounds small eggplants
Salt
1/4 cup mild olive oil
1/4 cup Pedroncelli Fume Blanc
1 pound white potatoes, peeled
Ground black pepper
1 pound onions, peeled
2 medium red, yellow or green bell peppers, cored & seeded
1 pound ripe tomatoes, cored
1 can (5 oz.) black pitted olives, drained, rinsed & halved

CHATEAU SOUVERAIN

CAFE AT THE WINERY
A UNIQUE FOOD AND WINE EXPERIENCE

LUNCH   FRI. SAT. SUN.   DINNER

Highway 101 to Independence Lane-Geyserville, CA   707-433-3141

RISOTTO WITH GRILLED FENNEL & CHATEAU CURED SALMON
Chateau Souverain

6 oz. center cut salmon
1/2 oz. kosher salt
1 oz. sugar
3 Tbsp. chopped dill
Ground pepper
Olive oil
5 cups fish stock
5 Tbsp. butter
1 1/2 cups Arborio rice

The salmon needs at least 3 days for preparation. Mix the salt and sugar together; lay the salmon, skin side down, on some clear wrap; pack the salt and sugar mixture on the salmon and wrap tight with the clear wrap, then in aluminum foil. Place on a plate in the refrigerator with about a one pound weight on top. After 2 days, open and place some fresh ground pepper, 2 teaspoons olive oil, and the chopped dill on top. Rewrap and return to the refrigerator with the weight on top. After the third day, the salmon may be sliced as needed.

Put the fish stock in a sauce pan to simmer. Melt the butter and sauté the onions, add the fennel seeds and arborio rice, stir for 2 minutes, add the wine and reduce at medium heat. The stock should be added 1/2 cup at a time, don't drown the rice. Attention should be paid to the heat—if the stock is reduced too fast, the risotto ends up soft on the outside and chalky in the middle. If reduced too slow, it becomes gluey.

The risotto should stop cooking when it is al dente (about 20 minutes). Also, the liquid you add may vary from time to time. Season the finished risotto and add the Parmesan. (For a slightly richer risotto, add 4 ounces of reduced cream.)

The fennel bulb should be sliced with the root holding the slice together, brushed with olive oil and grilled until cooked. Then cut out the root, leaving just enough to slice together.

Place the risotto in the middle of the plate (a small ring about 4" wide may be used to make a neat presentation). Place the grilled fennel slice on top and about three thin slices of the Chateau Cured Salmon around the side. Garnish with a sprig of fresh dill or fennel top.

Recommended wine: *Chateau Souverain Chardonnay.*

1/2 cup Parmesan cheese
1/2 medium onion, chopped
1/2 cup Chateau Souverain Chardonnay
Salt & pepper
1 fennel bulb
1/2 tsp. roasted and ground fennel seeds

SALMON AU BEURRE D'ESHALOTES
(Salmon with Shallot Butter)
La Gare Restaurant

4 6-oz. filets of salmon (preferably King)
1/4 tsp. salt
1/4 tsp. pepper
3/4 cup flour
3/4 cup dry white wine
1 tsp. chopped shallots
Dash of lemon juice
3/4 cup salted butter
1 Tbsp. demi-glaze vegetable oil

Sprinkle bottom sides of filets with salt and pepper.

NOTE: *Seasoning only the bottoms of the filets prevents black specks from detracting from the overall presentation.*) Coat the filets gently with flour, tap filets gently to remove any excess flour. Preheat oven to 350 degrees. Coat bottom of oven-proof sauté pan or large skillet with oil. Heat to high temperature. Place salmon, flesh side down, in pan. Sauté 1 to 2 minutes, turn salmon, and pour off excess oil. Add 1/4 cup wine, place lid on pan, and bake in oven about 5 minutes or until fish is three-quarters done.

Remove pan from oven and pour off excess oil. Add shallots, lemon juice, butter, demi-glaze, and remaining 1/2 cup wine to pan. Cook over medium heat, 2 to 3 minutes. Remove filets to 4 warm dinner plates or a serving platter. Finish sauce by swirling all ingredients in the pan over medium heat until they reduce enough to coat filets. Spoon sauce onto plates. Set filets on sauce. Serve with rice, asparagus, and carrots. Garnish with parsley in fluted lemon cup.

Serves 4.

SALMON WRAPPED IN LETTUCE LEAVES
Geyser Peak Winery

Cut salmon filet into 1" square pieces. Marinate in soy sauce, ginger, Chardonnay, sesame oil, and pepper. Wrap in blanched iceberg lettuce leaves, securing with toothpicks. Sear in hot pan on 2 sides for 30 seconds each to seal lettuce leaves, then remove toothpicks. Bake in 350 degree oven for 10 minutes, serve with Dipping Sauce.

Serve with Geyser Peak Chardonnay.

1 lb. salmon filet
1 head iceberg lettuce
2 Tbsp. soy sauce
1 Tbsp. ginger
1 Tbsp. sesame oil
Pepper
1/4 cup Chardonnay

DIPPING SAUCE
2 Tbsp. soy sauce
1 Tbsp. rice wine vinegar
1/4 cup Chardonnay
Slivered ginger

CHARDONNAY STEAMED CLAMS
Sonoma Mission Inn & Spa

In a hot sauce pan, add clams, garlic, and wine. Cover and steam until clams open. In a separate pan, steam mustard greens and vegetables until tender. Pour hot clam juice over the top. Place in bowl and arrange clams over the top. Garnish with a piece of grilled baguette.

40 oz. clams
10 oz. Chardonnay wine
4 garlic cloves, minced
4 oz. mustard greens, steamed
2 oz. vegetable julienned & steamed— carrots, squash, zucchini, red and yellow peppers
2 oz. baguette, grilled

POACHED TROUT
Landmark Vineyards

6 trout, whole, boned
2 onions, thinly sliced
9 Tbsp. butter
1 cup Chardonnay
1 cup broth
1 bay leaf
Salt and pepper to taste
2 cloves garlic, crushed
1/2 cup breadcrumbs

Sauté the onions in 3 tablespoons butter until they are soft. Add Chardonnay, water, broth, salt, pepper, bay, and garlic. Bring to a boil and heat for 10 minutes.

Add trout to the pan, reduce heat to simmer. Poach for at least 10 minutes, basting often. Sauté the breadcrumbs in the remaining butter until they are brown.

Arrange trout on a platter, pour 1 tablespoon poaching liquid over each fish, then pour the butter and breadcrumbs over all the fish.

Serves 6.

BARBECUED TROUT
Landmark Vineyards

2 large trout
2 whole onions, sliced
2 beefsteak tomatoes, sliced
1 tsp. lemon juice
1/4 cup Chardonnay
Garlic salt to taste
Salt and pepper to taste

Toss onions, tomatoes, and lemon juice with the Chardonnay. Add garlic salt, salt and pepper. Slice trout lengthwise and stuff with the mixture. Wrap each trout with aluminum foil to make a package, folding the foil so that steam cannot escape when placed on the grill. (The package may expand a little because of the steam inside.) Place on rack above hot coals. Steam in foil for 20-25 minutes, keeping grill lid closed (except to turn the trout once for even distribution of the heat; make sure not to spill the stuffing).

Serves 2.

FETTUCCINE, CHICKEN BREAST AND MUSHROOMS IN WHITE SAUCE
Hamburger Ranch

While fettuccine is cooking: In a 12" sauté pan on high, heat 4 Tbsp. of olive oil, add garlic, chicken, mushrooms and tomatoes. Sauté ingredients until cooked, add butter and cream. Bring to a boil. Add fettuccine to skillet, tossing fettuccine continuously. Add black pepper to taste. Reduce to creamy consistency.
   Garnish with parsley and black olives.
   Serves dinner for 2 or entree for 4.

6 ounces fettuccine, cook, drain, do not rinse

4 Tbsp. olive oil

4 cloves garlic

2 6-ounce boneless chicken breast (raw, skinned and diced)

2 handsful mushrooms, sliced

1 tomato, diced

1/4 cup butter

1 pint cream

Black pepper to taste

2 Tbsp. chopped parsley

8 large black olives

1 loaf Cousteux French bread

STUFFED GUINEA FOWL
John Ash & Co.

4 dressed Guinea fowl, approximately 2 1/2 pounds each

4 Tbsp. shallots, slivered

2 Tbsp. garlic, minced

2 oz. dried porcini mushrooms, rinsed well and rehydrated in 2 cups water with a big pinch of sugar

4 Tbsp. clarified butter or light olive oil

1 cup rich Guinea or chicken stock

2 large eggs

1 Tbsp. each, finely chopped: fresh parsley, thyme, and chives

2/3 cups each: walnuts, pecans and pistachios, chopped coarsely

Salt and freshly ground white pepper to taste

This dish was created by Jeff Madura, the very talented young chef at John Ash & Company restaurant in Santa Rosa, California. It works equally well with pheasant.

Sauté the shallots, garlic, and mushrooms in the butter until lightly colored. Add stock and reduce quickly so that most of the moisture is evaporated. Cool. Beat eggs and stir into mushroom mixture along with the herbs and nuts. Correct seasoning with salt and pepper.

Remove legs from the fowl and bone out to create a pocket. Season lighlty and stuff with a tablespoon or so of the nut mixture. Fold meat over to enclose stuffing then wrap in foil to hold shape.

Remove the breast from bone and split into two supremes. Remove the skin and any fat. Gently pound the breast between layers of waxed paper to 1/4 inch in thickness. Season lightly and roll up a tablespoon or so of the nut mixture. Wrap in plastic and carefully tie the ends into a sausage shape.

To Serve:

Place the legs on a rack in a roasting pan and roast in a preheated 400 degree oven for 12 minutes. While legs are cooking, poach the breasts in their plastic wrap in simmering water for 8-10 minutes. Remove plastic and foil wraps and place a breast and leg portion on eight warm plates. Garnish with lightly sautéed wild mushrooms and surround with Orange and Ginger Scented Sauce.

Orange and Ginger Scented Butter Sauce

Sauté shallots and mushrooms in a heavy 8 cup sauce pan with one tablespoon of the butter until golden brown. Add stock, wine, lemon juice and ginger, and reduce by half.

Add cream and reduce again by 1/3 or until large bubbles appear and mixture coats the back of a spoon. Strain, add orange zest and juice and correct seasoning. Sauce will hold for a couple of hours in a warm spot near the stove (not over 100 degrees) or in a thermos until serving time. Serves 8.

A crisp chardonnay is the recommended wine to be served with this dish.

3 Tbsp. shallot or green onion, minced

1/2 cup mushrooms, sliced

2 1/2 cups flavorful Guinea or chicken stock

2/3 cup Chateau DeBaun Pinot Noir

1 Tbsp. fresh lemon juice

2 Tbsp. fresh ginger, peeled and minced

2/3 cup heavy cream

6 Tbsp. unsalted butter

2 medium oranges, zested and juiced

Salt and freshly ground white pepper to taste

Wine is inspiring and adds greatly to the joy of living.

Napoleon (1769–1821)

FETTUCCINE WITH CHICKEN
The Restaurant

1 1/2 lbs. chicken breasts, skinned, cut into 1" to 1 1/2" cubes

Butter as needed

1/3 cup coarsely chopped walnuts

2 large onions, thinly sliced

3 large red bell peppers, cut into 1/4" julienne

8-9 asparagus spears, cut 1" diagonal and blanched—refresh in ice water

1 lb. dry fettuccine

1/4 tsp. freshly grated nutmeg

3/4 cup grated Parmesan cheese

Freshly ground black pepper

1 cup each: heavy cream and chicken stock

Toast walnuts in 1 tablespoon melted butter. Remove from pan with slotted spoon onto paper towel; set aside. In 1/2 cup melted butter with 1 tablespoon olive oil, sauté onions and bell peppers until onions are very soft; add asparagus. Add to vegetable mix: heavy cream, stock, and nutmeg. Bring to full boil: reduce heat to low, then set aside. Cook fettuccine al dente. Drain and keep warm. Sauté chicken in olive oil until golden brown and just done. Add pasta, chicken and Parmesan to vegetable sauce. Toss well. Season with pepper, garnish with toasted walnuts.

Serves 4.

THAI-STYLE CASHEW CHICKEN
The Restaurant

A simple dish, easy to prepare for 4-6 people. For each person 1 10-ounce chicken breast, skinned, trimmed, and halved is needed.

Slice chicken breast halves crossway into 6-8 slices. Heat 2-3 tablespoons peanut oil in sauté pan or wok. Add garlic, sauté for 1 minute. Add chicken and oyster sauce; sauté for 3 minutes or until chicken is just done. Add green onions, chilis, and cashews; mix well. Place lettuce leaf in a soup plate. Put chicken in lettuce leaf, rice to the side. If you are feeling ambitious, garnish with a green onion brush.

1 tsp. garlic, minced

3 fresh red "Bird" chilis or 3 dried red chili peppers

1/2 cup unsalted, roasted cashews (generous amount)

2 green onions, trimmed, and cut in 2" lengths

1 Tbsp. oyster sauce

Large Romaine leaf

1 cup steamed white rice

Wine is the most complicated fluid outside a blood vessel.

Salvatore Lucia, M.D. (1901-1984),
University of California School of Medicine

ROASTED GAME HENS ZINFANDEL
Sutter Home

2 Cornish game hens, about $1^{1}/_{4}$ lbs. each

2 tsp. dried, rubbed sage

2 tsp. dried chervil leaves

Salt and pepper

1 small orange

1 small apple, cored and quartered

4 Tbsp. butter or margarine, melted

2 Tbsp. light brown sugar, firmly pressed

$1^{1}/_{2}$ tsp. cornstarch

$^{1}/_{4}$ tsp. dry mustard

$^{1}/_{2}$ cup Sutter Home Red Zinfandel

Rinse hens and pat dry with paper towels. Season cavity of each hen with 1 teaspoon sage, 1 teaspoon chervil, salt and pepper. Cut orange in half lengthwise; reserve half—cut remaining half into 4 pieces. Stuff cavity of each hen with two orange pieces and two apple pieces; truss. Place hens on rack in small roasting pan. Baste with melted butter. Roast in a preheated 375 degree oven 1 hour, basting every 15 minutes. Hens are done when juices run clear when thigh is pricked. Meanwhile, with a vegetable peeler, remove zest from remaining orange half; cut zest into slivers. In a small saucepan combine zest with 1 cup water; bring to a boil and boil 1 minute. Drain, rinse, and set aside. In same saucepan, combine brown sugar, cornstarch and mustard, stir in wine. Cook, stirring constantly, until mixture thickens and boils. Remove from heat; stir in orange slices. Serve sauce with game hens.

Serves 2.

CORNISH GAME HENS GLAZED WITH PEPPER ORANGE SAUCE
Carol Hall, Hot Pepper Jelly Company

Remove the backbone from the game hens (this makes for easier handling at the table).

Salt and pepper each bird and roast whole. Bake at 350 degrees, uncovered, approximately 45 minutes or until thoroughly cooked.

When hens are cooked, remove from the oven. Pour the Red Pepper Orange Sauce over each bird and return to oven for 5 to 10 minutes. Serve piping hot. Serves 4.

4 Cornish game hens, approximately 1 1/2 lbs. each
Salt and pepper to taste
4 oz. Red Pepper Jelly
Juice from 1 whole orange
1 Tbsp. orange zest
1 Tbsp. freshly grated ginger (optional)

GRILLED BREAST OF CHICKEN WITH ORANGE-APRICOT GLAZE
Bandiera Winery

Combine all ingredients in a small saucepan. Stir over medium heat until preserves are melted and all ingredients are combined.

Grill the chicken breasts over medium hot coals for about 20 minutes. Cook for 10 more minutes, brushing with glaze four times while cooking.

Delicious with rice, steamed asparagus, and Bandiera Chardonnay.

4 chicken breasts

GLAZE

1/2 cup apricot preserves
1/4 cup orange juice
1 clove garlic, finely chopped or 1/4 tsp. garlic powder
1 Tbsp. ginger, finely chopped or 1 tsp. dried ginger
1/2 tsp. ground black pepper
1/2 tsp. salt

HOT PEPPER GLAZE
(For Chicken Breast or Pork Chops)
Carol Hall, Hot Pepper Jelly Company

2 Tbsp. Jalapeno Pepper Jelly

2 Tbsp. Red Pepper Jelly

2 tsp. hot sweet mustard

2 whole oranges, peeled and sliced

4 chicken breasts or pork chops

Combine jellies with mustard and orange slices.

Broil chops or chicken until done. Remove from oven, top with glaze, and return to oven. Broil until glaze is heated thoroughly, 3-5 minutes.

Serves 4.

POPPY HONEY CHICKEN
Carol Hall, Hot Pepper Jelly Company

1 chicken breast (per serving)

3 Tbsp. Poppy Honey Dressing (per chicken breast)

Salt and pepper to taste

1 bunch fresh spinach for two servings or 2 bunches fresh spinach for 4-6 servings

Olive oil (small amount)

Salt and pepper each chicken breast as desired. Arrange in ungreased baking dish and place in 350 degree oven. Cook until about half done (15-20 minutes). Remove from oven and pour Poppy Honey Dressing over each piece. Return to oven and finish baking (10-15 minutes). Do not over-cook.

Wash, drain, and dry spinach. Just before ready to serve chicken, quickly sauté spinach in small amount of oil just to heat (some leaves will still be crisp). Place equal amounts of spinach on each warm plate and top with chicken breast. Garnish with paprika.

GRILLED CHICKEN BREAST TOPPED WITH SUN-DRIED TOMATO PESTO
Fountaingrove Inn

Heat grill. For Pesto, place pine nuts, basil, Parmesan, olive oil, garlic, and pepper in food processor or blender container; cover, and process or blend until ingredients are chopped fine. Fold in sun-dried tomatoes with wooden spoon. Add salt to taste.

Brush chicken breasts with clarified butter. Grill, 4 inches above heat source, until done, about 5 minutes, basting with butter as necessary.

To serve, place chicken on plate and top with dollop of Sun-dried Tomato Pesto.

6 8-oz. each whole chicken breasts, boned and skinned

1 Tbsp. pine nuts

1 cup fresh basil leaves (or substitute 3/4 cup fresh parsley and 2 Tbsp. dried basil leaves)

2 Tbsp. Parmesan cheese

1/4 cup olive oil

2 large cloves garlic, peeled

1/4 tsp. ground white pepper

2 Tbsp. sun-dried tomatoes (oil packed), drained and chopped

Salt to taste

Clarified butter

I feast on wine and bread, and feasts they are.

Michelangelo (1475—1564)

TRADITIONAL ROAST GOOSE
John Ash, Fetzer Vineyard

1 6-8 lb. goose

1 lb. yellow or red onions

2 Tbsp. garlic, minced

1 oz. dried porcini or cepes mushrooms, rinsed well and soaked for 2 hours in water

2 cups dry French or Italian bread crumbs

1 cup milk, heated to lukewarm

1/8 cup fresh sage leaves, minced (2 Tbsp. dry)

4 Tbsp. fresh parsley, minced

Salt and freshly ground pepper

Freshly grated nutmeg

Optional: 3/4 cup chopped walnuts, filberts, diced celery, cooked and drained sweet sausage, or fresh chopped oysters, or a combination, can also be added to the stuffing

Farm-raised geese are quite fat and the key to a successful goose dish is the rendering of the fat. An easy way to do this is to prick the goose a few times, then steam the bird, covered, in a large pot for 45 minutes to 1 hour. Place the goose on a rack so it doesn't touch the water. The goose fat is highly prized in France to sauté with, especially potatoes. You may wish to save it for that purpose. Steam goose, if desired, to render some of the fat. Roast unpeeled onions in preheated 375 degree oven for 30 minutes, or until tender. Cool, peel, and chop. Drain and finely chop mushrooms. Sauté mushrooms and garlic in 1 tablespoon of rendered goose fat, or olive oil, until garlic is soft. Do not brown. Soak bread crumbs in milk, then squeeze dry. Combine bread with onions, mushroom mixture, sage, and parsley. Season to taste with salt, pepper, and nutmeg. Stuff goose with mixture and truss the cavity closed. Roast goose in 350 degree oven for 2 1/2 hours or until juices run clean when thigh is pricked with a fork. Defat the pan drippings with a little apple brandy, if desired, and pour over the goose.

Serve with a lighter style, fruity, red zinfandel or chilled gamay.

CHICKEN BREAST WITH BLEU CHEESE IN A ROSEMARY PEAR SAUCE
The Ledford House

Halve chicken breasts. Make a slit in the side of each half chicken breast and insert 1 ounce bleu cheese. Place in a baking pan, skin side up, and bake 20-25 minutes at 350 degrees or until flesh is firm.

Peel, core, and cut pears in chunks, cook over medium heat in 1 cup water with the rosemary. When pears are soft, remove the rosemary sprig and puree pears, juice and the wine. When mixture is smooth, salt to taste.

To serve, pour pear sauce on a plate, set chicken breasts on top, and garnish with rosemary.

Serves 6.

3 full chicken breasts
6 oz. bleu cheese
3 large D'Anjou pears
1/2 cup water
1/2 cup Greenwood Ridge Late Harvest Riesling
1 sprig rosemary
Salt

Wine was created from the beginning to make men joyful, and not to make men drunk. Wine drunk with moderation is the joy of the soul and heart.

Ecclesiastes 31:35

BUTTERMILK PECAN CHICKEN BREAST
Spring Street Restaurant

Deboned fresh breast of chicken
3 1/2 cups all-purpose flour
2 cups shelled pecans
1 tsp. salt
1 Tbsp. baking powder
1 cup buttermilk
2 egg yolks

In a food processor grind 1 cup of the pecans with 1/2 cup flour until the nuts are milled very fine (about 1 1/2 minutes), add the remaining flour, nuts, salt, and baking powder, and mix with short bursts (2-3 seconds) until the nuts are coarsely ground.

Separate two eggs and mix the yolks with 1 cup buttermilk.

Dredge the chicken breast (for best results pound breast to a uniform thickness) through all purpose flour, then dip into buttermilk mixture, and coat the breast well with the pecan flour. Sauté in olive oil until both sides are golden brown. Finish in oven at 350 degrees for 3-5 minutes (until done).

Garnish with homemade applesauce, sour cream, and cranberry chutney, or any tart berries, i.e., olallieberry, blackberry, boysenberry, etc.

COUNTRY CHICKEN PICCATA
Lincoln Avenue Grill

*Remove skin from chicken. Dredge in seasoned flour and sauté until golden brown. Put in preheated 350 degree oven for 15 minutes. Cook fettuccine as directed. Trim and blanch broccoli in boiling salted water. Reduce wine by 1/2; remove from heat and slowly add butter, 1 ounce at a time. Add capers and lemon juice. Warm plates. Place pasta in 4 equal servings on plates; place chicken on top and arrange broccoli around pasta. Cover all with sauce and garnish with chopped parsley.
Serves 4.*

4 8-oz. chicken breasts
1 lb. fettuccine pasta
2 large bunches broccoli
1 bottle dry white wine
1/4 lb. butter
Juice of 1/2 lemon
Capers

GRILLED CHICKEN BREAST WITH MERLOT SAUCE
St. Francis Vineyards

Rinse and pat dry chicken. Using a light olive oil and lemon mixture, baste chicken breasts while grilling until liquids run clear. (Do not overcook.) Remove chicken and keep warm.

*In large skillet, lightly sauté garlic and rosemary in olive oil. Add mushrooms, chicken stock and Merlot, and cook until reduced and somewhat syrupy. Add salt and pepper to taste. Add chicken and tomatoes to sauce until heated through. Arrange on platter topped with chopped parsley.
Serves 6.*

6 boned chicken breasts, skin removed
1/2 lb. mushrooms, sliced
1 1/2 cups Italian tomatoes, chopped
Olive oil
2-4 cloves garlic, minced
1-2 Tbsp. rosemary, crushed
1 cup chicken stock
1 cup St. Francis Merlot
Parsley, chopped
Salt and pepper (optional)

FETTUCCINE ALFREDO
Italian Affair

20 ounces fresh fettuccine
1/2 cup sweet butter
1 cup heavy cream
1/4 cup fresh Parmesan cheese, grated
Salt and pepper

Melt butter in large skillet. When it foams, add cream and simmer until slightly thickened. Season to taste with salt and white pepper. Turn off heat. Meanwhile, bring 1 1/2 gallons water to full boil. Add fettuccine and cook for 3-4 minutes, until tender. Drain. Add the pasta to the cream sauce and toss with the freshly grated cheese. Serve at once.

Serves 4.

GREENWOOD RIDGE VINEYARDS

· PICNIC GROUNDS ·

HOME OF THE
· CALIFORNIA WINE CHAMPIONSHIPS ·

Hours: Summer 10-6
Winter 10-5

5501 Highway 128 • Philo, CA 95466
(707) 895-2002

ZINFANDEL FENNEL TOMATO SAUCE
Dory Kwan, for Greenwood Ridge Vineyards

Enjoy this lively "one pot" sauce with your favorite pasta or even with polenta. It's a must with Greenwood Ridge Vineyards Zinfandel.

Put the onion, shallot, garlic, and parsley in blender with some of the tomato juice and puree. Add the pepper, some of the tomatoes (this may have to be done in two batches), and puree until smooth.

Heat a large pot until almost smoking. Add the olive oil and then the fennel. Stir until very brown. Empty the tomato puree into the pot with wine and bring to a boil. Reduce heat to medium and cook until the sauce is very thick. Stir occasionally with a wooden spoon. Taste sauce and add honey if necessary.

2 28-oz. cans whole tomatoes

1/2 onion, diced

5 cloves garlic

1 shallot

1 bunch parsley leaves

1 fennel bulb, finely minced (a food processor works well)

Fennel sprigs for garnish

1 Tbsp. olive oil

1/2 cup Greenwood Ridge Vineyards Zinfandel

1 tsp. salt

1-2 Tbsp. black pepper, freshly ground

1 Tbsp. honey (helps a lot if the tomatoes are very acidic)

POLENTA CASSEROLE
Sylvia Sebastiani, Sebastiani Winery

3 quarts water (reduce water if thicker polenta is desired) or use chicken broth
1 1/2 Tbsp. salt
3 cups polenta
4 Tbsp. butter
Grated Parmesan cheese
1 lb. Teleme cheese, shredded (optional)

SPAGHETTI SAUCE

1/2 cup dried Italian mushrooms, soaked in hot water, then chopped
1 28-oz. can solid pack tomatoes, mashed with liquid
1 lb. ground beef
4 Tbsp. olive oil
4 Tbsp. butter
4 stalks celery, chopped
4 onions, chopped
4 cloves garlic, finely chopped
1/4 tsp. thyme
1/4 tsp. rosemary
1/2 cup finely chopped parsley
6 8-oz. cans tomato sauce
1 1/2 cups red wine
1 cup dry white wine
1 tsp. sugar
Salt and pepper to taste

Bring water to a boil; add salt. Measure polenta into a bowl and gradually add to water, stirring constantly. Turn heat down and continue cooking for 50 minutes, stirring frequently. Butter a shallow casserole dish and spread half the polenta in bottom. Put Spaghetti Sauce and cheese over this, then spread another layer of polenta, again topping with sauce and cheese. Slices of teleme cheese can be used between the layers if desired. Bake in 375 degree oven for 30 minutes.

For the Spaghetti Sauce; If using meat, brown meat in olive oil and butter. Add celery and onions until brown, then add garlic. Salt and pepper to taste, then add spices, mushrooms with their liquid, tomatoes, and tomato sauce. Rinse tomato sauce cans with water and add to sauce along with wine and sugar. Cook for 3 hours over low heat, stirring occasionally. If not using meat, start by browning onions and celery and proceed as above.

Serves 6 to 8.

VITELLO CON FUNGHI E CREAMAS (Veal)
Italian Affair

Heat the oil in a large skillet. Salt and pepper the veal to taste and dredge lightly in flour, shaking off excess. Sauté each scallopine of veal until slightly brown on each side, 30 seconds to a minute. Do not overcook. Remove veal from pan and add the mushrooms to the same pan. Sauté until tender. Add the shallots, sauté one minute, deglaze the pan with the sherry. Add the cream and demi-glace, if it is to be used. Cook until slightly thickened. Adjust seasoning, return the veal and its juices to the pan, warm slightly, and then arrange the veal on the plate and pour the sauce over to serve.

12 slices veal, 1 1/2 oz. each, pounded

4 Tbsp. oil

Salt, pepper, and flour

1 pound wild oyster mushrooms, sliced

3 Tbsp. shallots, chopped

1/2 cup dry sherry

1 1/2 cup heavy cream

1/2 veal demi-glace (optional)

Back of this wine is the vintner, and back through the years, his skill; And back of it all the vines in the sun, and the rain, and the Master's will.

Anonymous

TRENTADUE TOURNEDOS
Trentadue Winery

4 lbs. veal, boned and tied, or 4 lbs. turkey breast, boned and rolled

Place meat in a six-quart kettle. Add 1 1/2 cups dry white wine, 1 bay leaf, 1 clove garlic (crushed), and enough water to cover meat. Bring to a boil, then lower heat and cover. Simmer until meat is very tender when pierced, or when meat thermometer inserted into thickest part registers 170 degrees (about 1 1/2 to 2 hours). Let meat cool in stock. Cover and chill.

For sauce, drain oil from 3-ounce can of tuna into measuring cup. Add light olive oil to make one cup. In a food processor or blender, combine tuna, 5 anchovy filets, 3 tablespoons lemon juice, 2 eggs and 1 1/2 tablespoons capers. Whirl until smooth.

Slowly add the oil, pouring in a steady stream until well blended. Cover and chill at least 4 hours.

When meat is cold, remove from stock and slice thinly. Pour 1/3 of sauce into bottom of large shallow dish. Arrange meat slices over top and cover with remaining sauce. Cover and chill at least 2 hours. Add lemon slices and more capers on top.

VEAL DIJONNAISE
(Sautéed Veal with Mustard Sauce)
La Gare French Restaurant

Season the veal with the salt and pepper and dredge in flour, removing the excess. Sauté the veal on both sides until it becomes golden brown. Remove the veal from the pan and place on a warm plate. Remove the oil from the pan; add the shallots, sliced mushrooms, mustard, and the wine. Bring to a boil and reduce. When wine is reduced by half, add the cream and again reduce by half. Arrange the veal on serving plates, rectify the seasoning and pour the sauce over the veal. Serve with rice or noodles.

Serves 2.

4 3-ounce scallops of veal

1 Tbsp. butter

1 Tbsp. oil

2 shallots, finely diced

1 Tbsp. Dijon mustard

1/4 cup dry white wine

1 cup heavy cream

1/2 cup sliced mushrooms

Salt and cayenne pepper

2 Tbsp. chopped parsley

Flour (to dust veal)

LEG OF LAMB WITH MUSTARD AND HERBS
The Ledford House

1 4-6 lb. leg of lamb, boned, butterflied, and trimmed

6 medium garlic cloves, peeled

2 tsp. each fresh thyme, oregano, sage, and rosemary

1/2 cup Dijon mustard

Salt and pepper

1 750-ml. bottle Cabernet Sauvignon

Preheat oven to 500 degrees. Lay leg flat, skinside down, and sprinkle with salt. In food processor, chop garlic and herbs until fine. Add to mustard. Spread mixture evenly over top of lamb. Sprinkle with pepper, then roll and tie. Place in baking pan, add wine to pan and bake at 500 degrees for 15-20 minutes. Turn oven down to 350 degrees and continue baking for 30 minutes more for rare. Remove roast from pan and allow to sit for 15 minutes. Reduce pan juices by half and serve over slices of lamb.

No one wine has been fully defined, molecular type by molecular type, as to its composition; happily so for the romantic.

*Vernon L. Singleton, Ph.D.,
Professor Emeritus, Enology, Universsity of California, Davis*

LAMB WITH CILANTRO/CUMIN CRUST
Chef Mary Evely, Simi Winery

Here's a recipe that definitely argues against the old rule of thumb of serving red wine with meat.

Clean the loins of all fat and silverskin. If the tenderloins are attached, clean them as well. Brush with olive oil and sprinkle with salt.

Puree the cilantro leaves in a food processor with the cumin and cayenne. Add olive oil a tablespoon at a time until mixture is the consistency of jam. Smear over the loins and set aside, covered, for 1/2 hour to 1 hour. (They may also be held overnight, refrigerated.)

Prepare a charcoal fire or preheat a gas grill.

Grill the loins for approximately 4 minutes per side for rare. (Times are approximate due to the variability of grill temperatures.) Meat should spring back to the touch, or use the sharp point of a knife to test for desired doneness. The smaller tenderloins will cook more quickly.

Let meat rest for a few minutes, then cut into slices and arrange on a warmed plate.

Serves 4.

2 whole lamb loins

Olive oil

1/2 bunch cilantro, stems removed

2 Tbsp. ground cumin

1/2 tsp. cayenne pepper

Salt to taste

Suggested wine: Simi Sauvignon Blanc

GRILLED MEDALLIONS OF VENISON WITH BLACKBERRY SAGE SAUCE
John Ash, Fetzer Vineyards

2 tsp. fresh sage, finely minced

1 Tbsp. shallot, finely minced

1/2 tsp. black pepper, freshly ground

4 5-oz. medallions of venison, cut from the loin

SAUCE

1/4 cup chopped shallots

2 Tbsp. olive oil

1 cup hearty red wine

1 cup rich game or veal stock

1 3/4-cup blackberries

2 Tbsp. sage leaves, freshly chopped

1-2 Tbsp. wild honey

Salt and freshly ground black pepper, to taste

Mix sage, shallot, and black pepper together and marinate venison 6 hours or refrigerate overnight.

To complete sauce: Sauté shallots in olive oil until light brown. Add wine and stock and reduce mixture to a light sauce consistency. Add berries, sage, and honey, and simmer over moderate heat for 10 minutes. Sauce should coat the back of a spoon. If not, raise heat and reduce further. Correct seasoning with salt and pepper, strain and keep warm.

Grill or broil medallions to rare or medium rare. Place medallions on warm plates and surround with sauce. Garnish with blackberries and sage sprigs.

Serves 4.

Mr. Ash suggests serving this with a hearty Fetzer Zinfandel.

GRATIN OF POLENTA, TOMATO FONDUE & SONOMA JACK
Sonoma Cheese Factory

For the polenta, melt butter in an oven proof pan. Sauté onions and add polenta. Pour boiling water and salt over. Place in 350 degree oven for 35-40 minutes. Stir and pour into oiled pan and spread out to 1/2" thick and smooth the top. Cool and cut into desired shape. This may be made up to 2 days ahead.

For tomato fondue, melt butter and olive oil over medium heat, sauté onions until translucent, about 3-5 minutes. Add remaining ingredients and simmer 20 minutes. Salt and pepper to taste.

To assemble, layer in a butter 12" gratin pan with shaved Dry Jack, Sonoma Jack, and tomato fondue. Drizzle with 1 cup cream. Bake at 350 degrees until golden brown and bubbly, about 30-40 minutes.

Serves 6.

4 Tbsp. butter

1/2 medium onion, minced fine

1 cup large cracked polenta

4 cups boiling water

1 Tbsp. kosher salt

1 tsp. large cracked black pepper

TOMATO FONDUE

1 Tbsp. butter

1/4 cup olive oil, extra virgin

1 clove garlic, minced

2 shallots, minced

1 1/2 lbs. tomato concassee (seeds and juice squeezed out)

1 Tbsp. tomato paste

1/4 California bay leaf

Salt and pepper to taste

1 Tbsp. sugar

WILD RICE SAGE DRESSING
Elaine Bell, Bandiera Winery

1 cup cooked wild rice
1 cup fresh white bread cubes
1/2 cup sweet butter or olive oil
1/2 cup diced yellow onions
1/4 cup grated carrots
1/4 cup diced celery
3 cloves chopped garlic
1 Tbsp. chopped fresh sage
1/4 cup Bandiera Chardonnay
1 egg, lightly beaten
1/4 cup heavy cream (optional)
Salt and pepper

Wild rice is a natural accompaniment for duck. I have lightened the dressing by adding fresh bread cubes and lots of vegetables. In my house we always end up creating two or three different dressings at Thanksgiving. This is one of my favorites.

Heat the butter in a large pot, add the onions and cook until soft. Stir in the carrots, celery, garlic, and sage and cook for 5 minutes over low heat. Pour in the wine and simmer for 3-4 minutes. Remove from heat and fold the wild rice and bread cubes into the vegetable mixture. Stir in the eggs and cream, then season with salt and black pepper. Turn into a greased 1 1/2 quart baking dish and cover with aluminum foil. Bake for 45 minutes at 375 degrees.

Serves 6.

I think it is a great error to consider a heavy tax on wines as a tax on luxury. On the contrary, it is a tax on the health of our citizens.

Thomas Jefferson (1743–1826)

SCALLOPED YAMS WITH PECANS
Elaine Bell, Bandiera Winery

Several years ago I decided that yams just didn't need any more sugar than they already had to offer. This recipe was inspired by my love for Pommes Boulangere which is a similar preparation using russet potatoes instead of yams and usually has a roast of meat or fish placed directly on the potatoes during the cooking time. These are delicious and show off the wonderful flavor and sweetness of yams.

Butter a 13" x 9" baking dish. Spread a layer of sliced yams on the bottom of the dish and sprinkle with onions and pecans. Drizzle 1/5 of the butter over the yams and season with salt and pepper. Repeat the process until you have 5 or 6 layers of yams. Cover the dish with foil and bake at 375 degrees for 1 hour.
Serves 6.

3 lbs. yams, sliced 1/8 inch thick

1 large white onion, cut in half and sliced thinly

1/2 cup pecans, chopped

3/4 cup sweet butter, melted

Salt and pepper

Wine was created from the beginning to make men joyful, and not to make men drunk. Wine drunk with moderation is the joy of the soul and the heart.

Ecclesiastes 31:35

RALO'S QUICK AND EASY VERSATILE SAUCE

Ralo Bandiera, Canyon Road

2 cans cream of mushroom soup
1 can water
1 medium onion, chopped fine
1 Tbsp. parsley, chopped fine
1 Tbsp. rosemary
4 oz. dry sherry
4 oz. Cheddar cheese
1 Tbsp. Worcestershire sauce
Salt and pepper to taste

Mix all ingredients in large pot and cook over medium heat for 20 minutes, stirring frequently. Serve over left-over meat, crab, or lobster chunks, or your favorite pasta.

Canyon Road Cellars is only one hour north of San Francisco on Highway 101. One of the highlights of any Sonoma County wine tour, this historic landmark is located in the heart of the world renowned Alexander Valley wine growing region. Visitors to Canyon Road enjoy wine tasting, a gift shop and country deli, picnic areas and lots of warm hospitality.

Open 10 to 5 daily.

CANYON ROAD

19550 GEYSERVILLE AVENUE
GEYSERVILLE, CA 95441
707-857-3417

PASTA BANDIERA
Ralo Bandiera, Canyon Road

In a 6 to 8 quart pan, bring 3 quarts water to a boil over high heat. Meanwhile, melt 3 tablespoons of the butter in a wide frying pan over medium-high heat. Add bell peppers and cook, stirring often, until limp (about 7 minutes). Remove from pan and set aside.

Melt remaining 3 tablespoons butter in pan, add scallops and cook, stirring, until opaque in center when cut (about 1 minute). Remove from pan and set aside. Pour in wine and boil, uncovered, until reduced by half (about 12 minutes). Stir in cream and boil,stirring often, until reduced by about a third (about 7 minutes).

Meanwhile, cook noodles in boiling water until al dente (3 to 5 minutes for fresh, 7 to 9 for dry). Drain and place in a warm bowl. Add sauce, peppers, and scallops; toss well. Serve on warm plates along with a green salad and the same type wine as was used in the sauce.

Serves 4.

6 Tbsp. butter or margarine

2 large red bell peppers (about 1/2 lb. each), stemmed, seeded, and thinly sliced lengthwise

2 cups dry white wine

1 lb. scallops, rinsed and dried and, if large, cut into quarters

1 1/2 cups half & half

8 oz. fresh or dry spinach noodles

JIM'S PASTA
The Restaurant

PER SERVING

1-2 Tbsp. olive oil

1 clove garlic, minced

1 heaping Tbsp. toasted pinenuts

1 strip bacon, sliced crossways, fried crisp, drained

2 large prawns, peeled, deveined, each cut crossways into 4 pieces, dusted with Cajun seasoning to taste

A nice handful of Rodiatore pasta, cooked al dente

Parmesan cheese

Heat olive oil in sauté pan. Over moderate high heat, sauté prawns first until pink, 1-1½ minutes. Add all other ingredients except pasta; sauté until garlic is softened. Toss with drained pasta. Top with generous amount of grated Parmesan cheese.

Because our universe of study concerns a social problem, there is danger in singluar explanations of human behavior when placed in the hands of political bodies.

Kaye Middleton Fillmore, Ph.D., Sociologist,
University of California, San Francisco

RAVIOLI IN A LEMON CREAM SAUCE
Ristorante Piatti

Mix flours in pasta extruder; add eggs, oil and salt, slowly.

Combine all filling ingredients.

For sauce, heat cream to a boil. Add zest, juice, Parmesan, white pepper and salt. Return to boil. Remove from heat and strain through fine sieve.

Serve with fresh ground pepper.

1/2 lb. flour

1/4 lb. Semolina flour

3 eggs

1/4 tsp. olive oil

1/4 tsp. salt

Filling

1/2 lb. Ricotta

2 tsp. Parmesan

1/4 lb. spinach, cooked and pureed with a pinch of nutmeg, salt and pepper to taste

Sauce

1 pint heavy cream

Zest and juice of 1 1/2 lemons

5 Tbsp. Parmesan

1/4 tsp. white pepper

1/4 tsp. salt

PASTA ALL'ARRABBIATA
(Mad Pasta)
Trentadue Winery

1 8-oz. pkg. Mendocino Pasta Co. Garlic and Basil Fettuccine (cooked with 1 Tbsp. salt added to water, optional)

4 to 8 cloves minced fresh garlic (or even a whole bulb)

2/3 cube butter or margarine

1 to 2 finely diced dried red chili peppers

2 Tbsp. Fusano California Valley extra virgin olive oil

6 Sonoma brand dried tomatoes in olive oil

Approximately 3 oz. grated Parmesan cheese

Sauté minced garlic in butter. Add diced tomatoes at end just to heat. In separate skillet, heat olive oil to very hot. Add diced red chilis and cook, stirring constantly until they turn dark. When pasta is cooked to desired texture, drain well (do not rinse), and place in pre-warmed bowl large enough for tossing. Pour garlic mixture over and toss quickly. Add chili mixture and toss again. Toss once more with Parmesan cheese and salt to taste.

Serve with tossed green salad, fresh, crusty French bread, and a bottle of Trentadue's 1986 Carignane served at cellar temperature (60 degrees).

PASTA PUTTANESCA FRESCA
(Tuscan Style Fresh Tomato/Olive Salsa)
Michael Hirschberg, Ristorante Siena

Combine all the ingredients, allow to marinate at least 1 hour. Toss into freshly cooked pasta. This sauce also works well as a cold pasta salad dressing. Recipe yields approximately 1 1/2 gallons.

10 lbs. red and yellow tomatoes, peeled, seeded, diced

2 1/2 cups pitted black olives, coarsely chopped

20 anchovy filets, rinsed and chopped into a paste

1 cup capers

2/3 cup Italian parsley, chopped

1/4 cup raw garlic, minced into a paste

1 level Tbsp. red chili flakes (be careful!)

2 cups virgin olive oil

In our society wine is clearly considered the beverage of choice for integrative social occasions. Its use is associated with sociability and is almost always moderate in nature.

David J. Pittman, Ph.D., Sociologist, Washington University

ORANGE-COATED PORK LOINS
Helaine (Mrs. Louis M.) Foppiano

1 cup soy sauce
1 cup white wine
4 cloves garlic
1 Tbsp. grated fresh ginger
3 Tbsp. frozen orange juice concentrate
3 Tbsp. frozen cranberry juice or cran-apple juice concentrate

Marinate 2 to 4 pork loins up to 12 hours. Place loins in baking pan, add 1 to 2 cups of marinade.

For coating, blend 2 to 3 whole oranges (with skins) until no lumps remain but not too much liquified. Spoon over meat and spread evenly.

Bake at 325 to 350 degrees (until meat thermometer reads 185 degrees).

May be served warm with canned black cherries or chilled orange slices.

FOPPIANO
Vineyards

FOPPIANO
Vineyards
Petite Sirah
Sonoma County
ALC. 13% BY VOL.

Memorable
Reds!

Come and experience Foppiano's Petite Sirah, Zinfandel, Merlot and Cabernet—reds which *will* stand the test of time!
Healdsburg, Sonoma County, (707) 433-7272   Open Daily: 10-4:30

FOPPIANO CHRISTMAS RAVIOLI
Della Foppiano

Boil chicken with quartered onions and carrots; take meat off bone and grind. Chop onion, parsley, garlic, basil, celery leaves, and thyme. Sauté in olive oil. Drain spinach and grind. Add spinach to ingredients in olive oil and simmer over low to medium heat, stirring, for approximately 15 minutes or until mushy. Add to chicken. Add eggs to sticky consistency. Add cheese and season to taste with salt and pepper.

Using basic egg pasta dough, roll out a large round of dough. Cover with ravioli filling and cover with a second round of dough. Using a ravioli rolling pin, roll over the dough to make the squares. Cut apart and seal edges with zigzag ravioli cutter. Boil in generous amount of salted water for 10 to 15 minutes until tender when pricked with a fork. Cover with spaghetti sauce and serve.

2 cups spinach, chopped
4 cloves garlic
1/2 large onion
1/2 cup parsley
Pinch basil
1/4 cup celery leaves
1 tsp. thyme and/or oregano
2 Tbsp. olive oil
6 eggs
1/2 cup Parmesan cheese
1 tsp. salt
1/2 tsp. pepper
1 chicken
2-3 carrots, quartered
1-2 onions, quartered

HOT PASTA PRIMAVERA
Plaza Grill

1 bunch broccoli flowerettes
1 bunch cauliflower flowerettes
3 carrots, thin diagonal slices
3 zucchini, thin diagonal slices
1 cup mushrooms, sliced
1 cup bell pepper, sliced
4 green onions, sliced
4 oz. butter or oil
1 1/2 oz. each: Parmesan, Romana, Jack, or any cheese of choice
2 cups garlic cream sauce (Bechamel Sauce)
8-12 oz. fresh egg fettuccine
Parsley

GARLIC CREAM SAUCE
3 oz. butter or oil
3 oz. flour
2 cups warm milk (whole, lowfat, skim or half & half)
2 cloves garlic, chopped
Salt to taste

Blanch broccoli, cauliflower, carrots, and zucchini in hot water for 2 minutes. Sauté mushrooms, peppers, and green onions in butter or oil for 2-3 minutes. Add blanched vegetables to sautéed mixture and cook 2 more minutes. Add 1/3 cup white wine, if desired, and cook 1 minute. Add Garlic Cream Sauce and cook 3 more minutes.

Cook fettuccine 3-5 minutes in boiling salted water until desired doneness. Add to vegetable and cream sauce. Add cheese and cook until cheese is melted. Garnish, serve, and top with additional Parmesan and parsley.

Garlic Cream Sauce:
Melt butter or oil in heavy saucepan. Add flour to fat to make a roux. Cook, stirring, until slightly browned. Add warm milk and stir constantly until cream sauce is thickened. Add garlic and stir, cooking several more minutes. Salt to taste. If too thick, thin with additional milk, cream or white wine.

Serves 4.

PASTA WITH PEPERONATA SAUCE
Foppiano Vineyards

Roast peppers under a broiler or over a gas flame until skin blackens. Place in a paper bag for a few minutes, then remove peel under running water. This step can be omitted, but it enhances the flavor wonderfully.

Cut peppers into thin strips. Meanwhile, sauté onion and garlic in olive oil until soft, then add pepper strips and continue to cook, stirring often, for another 10 minutes.

Bring to boil 3 quarts or so of water to cook pasta. Add to water 1 tablespoon each, oil and salt.

Quarter tomatoes and cook over low heat until soft. Pass through a food mill or strainer and add puree to peppers and onions. Add basil, wine, and salt, and continue to cook another 10 or 15 minutes over medium heat, stirring often, until mixture is reduced to 3 cups. Meanwhile, add pasta to boiling water and cook until tender. Drain and combine with pepper, tomato sauce, capers, and Parmesan cheese. Serve immediately.

4 SERVINGS

4 large or 6 medium bell peppers, red, green, and yellow if available

1 large white onion, slivered

2 or 3 cloves garlic, crushed

1/4 cup olive oil

1 pound ripe tomatoes

1 tablespoon fresh basil leaves, chopped, or 1 teaspoon dried

1/2 cup red wine

1 teaspoon salt

1/4 cup grated Parmesan cheese

1 tablespoon capers, optional

12 ounces whole wheat spaghetti or linguini, preferably durum

BLACK BEAN CHILE
Margaret Fox, Cafe Beaujolais

4 cups black beans

2 Tbsp. cumin seeds

2 Tbsp. Beaujolais Blend Herbs (or oregano)

2 large finely-chopped yellow onions

1 1/2 cups finely-chopped green bell peppers

1 clove garlic, minced

1/2 cup olive oil

1 tsp. cayenne pepper

1 1/2 Tbsp. paprika

1 tsp salt

3 cups canned, crushed whole tomatoes

1/3 cup finely chopped jalapeno chilis (canned are fine)

1/2 lb. Monterey Jack or Cheddar cheese, grated

2/3 cup sour cream

1/2 cup green onions, finely chopped

8 sprigs cilantro (more to sprinkle on top)

Sort through the beans and remove the funky ones and the small pebbles that are always there. Rinse beans well. Place in a large pot and cover with water to several inches above the top. Cover and bring to a boil. Reduce the heat and cook for 1 3/4 hours or until tender. You will need to add more water if you start to see the beans.

When the beans are cooked, strain them. Reserve 1 cup of the cooking water and add it back to the beans.

Place the cumin seed and Beaujolais Blend Herbs (or oregano) in a small pan and bake at 325 degrees for 10 to 12 minutes until the fragrance is toasty.

Sauté the onions, green peppers, and garlic in the oil with the toasted cumin seed and herbs, cayenne pepper, paprika, and salt for 10 minutes or until the onions are soft. Add the tomatoes and chilies. Add this mixture to the beans and stir.

To serve, place 1 ounce grated cheese, then 1 1/4 cups hot chile in a heated bowl. Put a spoonful of sour cream on top of chile. Sprinkle with 1 tablespoon green onions and place a sprig of cilantro in the sour cream. Optionally, sprinkle chopped cilantro to taste on top.

CASSOULET FROM PUY
Fred Halpert, Brava Terrace

Sauté carrot, onion, and celery in olive oil over medium heat. Add lentils, bay leaf, and thyme and sauté one minute.

Add chicken stock, bring to a boil, cover, and cook for 15 minutes (on medium heat) or until lentils are al dente, stirring occasionally. Remove from heat and set aside.

Cut the lamb and pork loin in half. Season with salt and pepper. Sear in hot skillet until well browned and still rare. Remove lamb and pork and sear sausages.

Sauté mushrooms separately with butter.

Quarter lamb and pork pieces. Cut sausages in half.

Return lentils to heat. Add all ingredients to lentils and cook until meat reaches desired degree of doneness (2 minutes rare; 4 minutes medium; 6 minutes well-done). Season to taste.

Add chopped chives for garnish and portion into 8 individual serving bowls.

Serves 8.

16 oz. lentils, preferably green from Puy

1 carrot, diced

1 medium onion, diced

2 celery stalks, diced

1 bay leaf

2 sprigs thyme

1 1/4 cups chicken stock

1/4 cup olive oil

1 lb. pork loin

1 lb. duck, venison, or other

1 lb. link sausage

1 lb. trimmed leg of lamb

Salt and white pepper

1 lb. mushroom, quartered

2 Tbsp. unsalted butter

1 bunch chives

BUTTERFLIED FILET OF BEEF WITH HERBS
Alice Waters

2 lbs. beef tenderloin, trimmed of fat and connective tissue

Salt and pepper to taste

3 Tbsp. finely chopped parsley

2 Tbsp. finely chopped chervil (1 tsp. dried)

2 tsp. finely chopped fresh thyme (1 tsp. dried)

2 Tbsp. vegetable oil

Have your butcher butterfly the beef tenderloin. Or you can do it yourself by cutting about 1¾" deep down the length of the filet. Roll back cut edge. Continue with knife tip pointing down, making sawing motions while pushing the knife sideways. Support the beef opposite the knife while cutting. When done, it should be about ¾" thick. Lay flat and press meat to even out thickness. Season with salt and pepper. Combine herbs; spread evenly over beef. Roll beef tightly, tying snugly with kitchen string at one-inch intervals. Bring to room temperature before cooking. heat oven to 425 degrees. In a large oven-proof skillet or roasting pan, heat oil over medium-high heat. Place roast in skillet, brown on all sides (about 4 minutes per side). Place roasting rack in skillet and place roast on rack. Do not cover. Insert meat thermometer in the thickest part of the roast.

Place in oven and roast until meat thermometer registers 135 degrees for rare, 155 degrees for medium (allow 10 to 12 minutes per pound for rare). Roasts will usually increase about 5 degrees after removal from oven. Remove to a cutting board and let "rest" in a warm place about 15 minutes. Remove string and carve. Serves 6.

Ms. Waters suggests serving with a salad of red onion, fennel and oranges on baby greens, dressed with a fruity olive oil and a touch of Balsamic vinegar. Grilled red peppers, onions and zucchini make a delightful side dish. Cabernet Sauvignon is the perfect complement.

HOLIDAY ROAST
Margaret Fox, Cafe Beaujolais

Preheat oven to 500 degrees. Mix together all ingredients (except meat). Place meat in a pan at least 9"x13" and spread herb mixture over entire surface, top and bottom. Bake for 15 minutes, then turn temperature to 300 degrees. Bake for about 45 minutes more, until internal temperature reads 125 degrees (medium rare). Remove from oven and let sit, covered with foil and in a warm place, for about 30 minutes.

4 lb. piece top sirloin, tied and allowed to sit outside refrigerator for 2 hours

3 Tbsp. corn or peanut oil

1 Tbsp. chopped fresh oregano

2 Tbsp. chopped fresh thyme

3 Tbsp. chopped fresh parsley

1 tsp. salt

1/4 tsp. ground pepper

Drink a glass of wine after your soup and you steal a ruble from your doctor

Russian Proverb

SAVORY STEAKS WITH SUN-DRIED TOMATO TOPPING
Bandiera Winery

4 8-oz. steaks
3 cloves garlic
1/2 cup parsley, chopped
2 Tbsp. olive oil
1 Tbsp. salt
2 tsp. black pepper

SUN-DRIED TOMATO TOPPING

1/4 cup sliced stale French bread, remove crust and cut in 1/2 inch cubes

1/2 cup sliced stale French bread: remove crust and crumble into small pieces

2 cloves garlic, chopped or 1 teaspoon garlic powder

1/4 cup sun-dried tomatoes, chopped

2 tsp. dried oregano or 2 tsp. fresh oregano chopped

2 Tbsp. olive oil

1 tsp. salt

1/2 tsp. ground black pepper

Combine all ingredients in a small bowl. Rub each steak on both sides with mixture. Let stand 20 minutes in refrigerator. Grill to desired doneness.

Toss all ingredients together in a mixing bowl. Spread in a thin layer on a cookie sheet. Place in a 300 degree oven for 5 minutes. Stir and return to oven for 5 minutes. Repeat this process until crumbs are toasted. Serve at room temperature over steaks.

Delicious with Bandiera Cabernet Sauvignon.

HASENPFEFFER
Gretchen and Randy Newman, Cazanoma Lodge

Cover rabbit with dry white wine and let marinate overnight.

Place rabbit in container with the rest of the ingredients, except for the sour cream.

Remove rabbit from marinade, roll in flour, and brown in searing pan. Place rabbit in roasting pan, cover with marinade and water. Bake 2 hours.

Remove rabbit from sauce mixture. Place sauce in pan. Heat, thicken with rue. Mix sour cream to taste. Place over rabbit and serve.

Serves 3.

One 3 to 3 1/2 pound rabbit cut into 9 pieces

10 dashes Tabasco Sauce

1 Tbsp. salt

1/2 tsp. pepper

3 bay leaves

1 lemon, juice and rind

1/2 tsp. ground pickling spice

1/4 tsp. thyme

Sour cream, to taste

MAGIC CHOCOLATE CAKE

1 3/4 cups unsifted all purpose flour
1 cup granulated sugar
1 cup brown sugar
3/4 cup Peter Rabbit's Cocoa Powder*
2 tsp. baking soda
1 tsp. baking powder
1 tsp. salt
2 eggs
1 cup black coffee
1 cup sour milk**
1/2 cup vegetable oil
1 tsp. vanilla

Combine dry ingredients in large mixing bowl. Add remaining ingredients. Beat at medium speed 2 minutes (batter will be thin). Pour into a greased and floured 13" x 9" x 2" pan. Bake at 350 degrees for 35 to 40 minutes or until cake tester comes out clean. Cool completely, frost.

*Cocoa Powder may be purchased by calling 1-800-4-R-CANDY.

**To sour milk, use 1 tablespoon vinegar plus milk to equal 1 cup.

DESSERTS

Use a little wine for thy stomach's sake.

Timothy 5:23

CHOCOLATE FRANGELICO CHEESECAKE
Alan Kantor, MacCallum House Restaurant

FILLING

8 oz. semi-sweet chocolate

2 lbs. cream cheese

1 1/2 cups sugar

1 cup sour cream

2 whole eggs

2 egg yolks

2 oz. Frangelico (hazelnut liqueur)

CRUST

2 oz. sweet butter

3/4 cup sourdough bread crumbs

GANACHE

5 oz. semi-sweet chocolate

3 oz. cream

1 oz. Frangelico

1/2 Tbsp. corn syrup

For filling, melt chocolate in double boiler. In food processor or mixer cream together the cream cheese and sugar until smooth. Add the sour cream, eggs, egg yolks, and Frangelico and mix well. Add melted chocolate and mix well.

Butter a 10" spring form pan liberally. Sprinkle bread crumbs around pan. Shake the pan to cover entirely with crumbs. Dump out excess. Pour in filling and bake in preheated 350 degree oven on the bottom shelf for 35 minutes. Cool at room temperature for about an hour before covering with ganache.

NOTE: It is very important that oven is 350 degrees; check with oven thermometer.

For the ganache, finely chop the chocolate and place in a bowl. In a small saucepan put the cream, Frangelico and corn syrup, bring to a simmer. Immediately pour the mixture over the chocolate and whisk until there are no lumps. Pour chocolate over center of cake, letting it run toward side of cake, trying to leave a 1" ribbon without ganache around outside edge. Place cake in refrigerator, preferably overnight.

Serves 12.

TIRAMI SU (Lift Me Up)
J. Pedroncelli Winery

Preheat oven to 350 degrees. Butter, or line with parchment, a 14"x9" pan. (Pan can be smaller or larger by 1-2 inches.) Beat yolks in clean bowl until soft peaks; add sugar and beat until stiff. Beat whites until stiff and fold into yolks, then fold in flour. Pour into prepared pan and bake about 20 minutes or until lightly colored and cake springs back to touch. Cool. Flip out and cut into 3 layers. For filling, beat yolks to break up and blend. Stir in mascarpone, sugar, and Grand Marnier.

For topping, warm chocolate by rubbing finger across an edge. Scrape a vegetable peeler across same edge. If chocolate is too cool, you'll get chocolate flakes. Warmer chocolate yields curls. Make curls right on top of assembled cake.

To assemble, layer into a 14"x9" pan: 1 cake layer, brush on 1/3 of Kahlua mixture, 1/3 mascarpone mixture spread thinly and evenly, and repeat process for next two layers ending with mascarpone. Cover thoroughly with chocolate curls. Chill for 3-4 hours to set. Cut into desired servings. Serve with fruit, creme anglaise (plain or flavored with Kahlua, espresso, or Grand Marnier), whipped cream or a la natural.

Serves 20.

CAKE
4 egg yolks
1 tsp. vanilla
1/4 tsp. salt
6 egg whites (3/4 cup)
2/3 cup sugar
2/3 cup sifted flour
8 egg yolks
2 1/2 packages (17 1/2 oz. each) mascarpone cheese
1/2 cup sugar, or to taste
3-4 Tbsp. Grand Marnier, or to taste

SOAKING LIQUID
2/3 cup espresso or strong coffee
1/3 cup Kahlua

TOPPING
8 oz. semi-sweet chocolate bar

BOURBON AND KENWOOD WALNUT TART
Charles Saunders, Eastside Oyster Bar & Grill

Tart Shell

2 cups all-purpose flour
1/2 tsp. salt
12 Tbsp. unsalted butter, cold
7 Tbsp. water, very cold
1/2 tsp. lemon zest, finely chopped

Nut Filling

8 oz. sugar
6 large, whole eggs
3 oz. dark corn syrup
2 oz. Wild Turkey bourbon
1 oz. unsalted butter, melted
1 tsp. vanilla extract
5 oz. Kenwood walnuts, roughly chopped
1/4 cup apricot jam, warm
1/8 cup water

In a large stainless steel bowl, sift all salt and flour together. Break cold butter into walnut size pieces and incorporate into flour. Pour in water and add zest. Work the mixture with a minimum amount of strokes (add more flour, if necessary) to form the dough. Remove from bowl and press into a flat, oblong shape, wrap in plastic, and refrigerate for several hours. Preheat oven to 325 degrees.

Using half the dough, roll out to desired thinness, place in tart shell and prick with a fork. Allow to rest for 30 minutes in the refrigerator. Prebake shell until light color forms (approximately 6 to 8 minutes).

In a bowl combine all ingredients for nut filling (except nuts). Sprinkle chopped nuts on base of prebaked tart shell. Pour in nut filling until it reaches the rim of the tart. Place immediately in a 350 degree oven and bake until the mixture is set (approximately 20 minutes). Remove tart from oven and brush with warm apricot jam, which has been thinned with water. Allow to cool and serve. Makes one 10" tart.

RUSSIAN CREAM WITH WILD HUCKLEBERRIES
Whitegate Inn

In small pan blend sugar, gelatin, and water. Let stand 5 minutes. Bring to a boil. Remove from heat and add cream. Mix sour cream and vanilla together, then gradually beat into sugar mixture.

Using parfait glasses alternate cream and berries, or mold in 4 cup container. Cover with plastic wrap. Chill 4 hours. Serve with additional berries, if desired.

3/4 cup sugar

1 envelope plain gelatin

1/2 cup whipping cream

1 1/2 cup sour cream

1 tsp. vanilla

1 cup huckleberries or other berries

SWEDISH APPLE CAKE
Gowan's Oak Tree, Philo

Cream sugar and shortening. Add beaten eggs, salt. Add flour, spices and soda. Mix in apples and nuts last. Pour into greased and floured baking pan. Bake 25 minutes at 350 degrees. For topping, combine 3 tablespoons melted butter, 3 tablespoons flour, 1 cup brown sugar, and spread at once over hot cake. Return to oven for another 25 minutes.

1 cup sugar

1/2 cup shortening

1/2 tsp. salt

1 tsp. cinnamon

1/4 tsp. cloves

1 tsp. soda

2 eggs

1 1/2 cups flour

3 cups raw chopped apples

1/2 cup nut meats

The Perfect Ending To A Great Meal

Sometimes it's better to let others do the talking....

"It's worth a special trip just to eat here." — *Travel & Leisure*
"The best of the new Wine Country style." — *Gourmet*
"Extraordinary food with no-punches-pulled flavor." — *Bon Appetit*

THE GRILLE
SONOMA MISSION INN & SPA
For reservations call (707) 938-9000, ext. 415

SPA COFFEE ICE CREAM
Sonoma Mission Inn & Spa

12 eggs
1 1/2 cups sugar
2 cups corn syrup
6 Tbsp. vanilla
1/2 tsp. salt
4 cups dry milk
48 oz. evaporated milk
10 cups milk
1 cup instant coffee
1/2 cup Kahlua

Mix eggs and sugar together in a large bowl; whisk until well combined. Mix dry milk with 5 cups milk until blended and whisk into egg and sugar mixture. Heat remaining milk and evaporated milk in a large sauce pan. Bring milk to a boil, add coffee and mix until dissolved. Add 1/2 of the hot milk in sauce pan. Stir hot milk and egg mixture over low heat until thick enough to coat the back of a spoon. (Be sure to stir with a rubber spatula, scraping bottom of sauce pan.)

Remove mixture from heat and add corn syrup, vanilla, and salt. Mix well. Place in an ice bath until well chilled. Add Kahlua and run through ice cream machine.

LEMON CHIFFON STRAWBERRY SAUCE
Sonoma Mission Inn & Spa

For the lemon chiffon, heat 2 tablespoons water with lemon zest; allow to steep for a few minutes and then strain, reserving lemon essence. Dissolve gelatin in lemon juice, heating slightly if necessary to completely dissolve gelatin. Whip eggs and sugar at high speed until light and thick, then add gelatin and lemon essence. Fold yogurt into egg mixture. Pour lemon chiffon into shell-shaped molds and freeze until set.

For strawberry sauce, place all ingredients in saucepan, heat until strawberries are softened. Pass through fine-holed strainer; adjust sweetness and reserve for service.

To assemble, run bottom of mold under hot water until chiffons slide out easily. Place on plate and spoon sauce around chiffon.

3/4 Tbsp. unflavored gelatin
2 eggs
1/4 cup sugar
1/8 cup lemon juice
1 tsp. lemon zest
2 Tbsp. water
3/4 cup plain, lowfat yogurt

STRAWBERRY SAUCE
1/2 pint strawberries
1 Tbsp. fructose
2 Tbsp. water
2 Tbsp. white wine

Wine is the nurse of old age.

Galen, 2nd Century A.D.

FRUIT TART WITH NUT CRUST
Heidi Cusick, Cookin' In

Pastry
1/3 cup almonds, pecans, walnuts, hazelnuts
1 1/4 cups flour
3 Tbsp. sugar
4 oz. chilled, unsalted butter
1 egg, separated
1-2 Tbsp. almond liqueur or water

Almond Paste Filling
7 oz. almond paste
2 Tbsp. powdered sugar
1 egg white
1 Tbsp. softened butter

Fruit & Glaze
Cherries, strawberries, peaches, nectarines, kiwi, raspberries, blackberries, blueberries, pears, apples (sliced & sautéed until just tender)
3/4 cup apple or red currant jelly with 1 Tbsp. fruit liqueur

Place nuts in food processor and process until ground. Add flour and sugar and mix. Cut butter into pieces and drop into flour. Pulse until butter is mixed in. Add yolk and liquid, pulse just to mix. Pour into 11" removable bottom tart pan and press gently to evenly distribute crust up sides and over bottom. Place in freezer for 10 minutes.

Preheat oven to 375 degrees. Bake tart shell 25 minutes or until lightly browned. Meanwhile, beat egg white until frothy. Brush over tart shell and return to oven for 1 minute. Combine all ingredients and mix well.

NOTE: If using this filling, omit the egg white on the tart and add it to the filling.

Spread the filling on while the tart is hot and place in oven 1 minute. Cut fruit and arrange on top of almond paste filling. Melt jelly with the liqueur and boil for 2 minutes. Let cool slightly, then pour, or brush over fruit arranged on tart. Refrigerate until 1 hour before serving.

Serves 8-10.

CHOCOLATE MACADAMIA NUT PIE
The Farmhouse Inn

Preheat oven to 350 degrees.

Melt chocolate and butter together over low heat, carefully, as not to burn. After melted, lightly stir together and set aside to cool slightly. In a mixing bowl, combine eggs, sugar, and salt. Mix on slow to medium speed or until mixture is smooth and combined. Add chocolate mixture and 1 1/2 cups nuts. Continue to mix at medium speed for 2 minutes. Pour into pie shell. Generously sprinkle remaining nuts on top. Bake for about 30 minutes or until pie sets up like custard. Let cool, but best served still warm with vanilla ice cream.

2 cups coarse chopped macadamia nuts
3 oz. unsweetened chocolate
4 eggs
1 cup sugar
6 Tbsp. butter
Pinch of salt
9" deep dish pie crust

Wine is the intellectual part of a meal, meats are merely the material part.

Alexander Dumas (1802–1870)

CHOCOLATE SILK
The Restaurant

3 oz. walnuts, toasted and coarsely chopped

4 oz. pecans, toasted and coarsely chopped

1/2 cup brown sugar, firmly packed

1 pinch ground cinnamon

4 oz. (1 stick) butter, melted

9" springform pan

MOUSSE CAKE

20 oz. bittersweet chocolate, cut into small pieces

6 oz. (1 1/2 sticks) soft butter

3/4 cup sugar

6 large eggs

1/4 cup heavy cream

1/2 tsp. vanilla

TOPPING

1 cup heavy cream

2 Tbsp. sugar

In a stainless steel bowl combine walnuts and pecans with brown sugar and cinnamon, stir in melted butter. Press nut mixture in bottom of pan, chill for 1/2 hour, or until firm.

For the cake, melt chocolate in double boiler. While chocolate is melting, combine butter and sugar in mixer; cream on medium speed until mix is light and fluffy. Switch to whisk attachment; add eggs, 2 at a time, mixing well after each addition. Scrape side of bowl; increase to medium high speed and whip for 2 minutes, until egg mixture increases lightly in volume. Whisk melted chocolate until it has cooled. It should be warm, not hot. Whisk chocolate into egg mixture on medium low speed. Scrape sides and bottom of bowl and continue to mix until chocolate is fully incorporated. Stir in cream and vanilla. Spread mousse filling in springform pan on top of crust. Chill until firm—6 hours to overnight.

Whip and spread evenly over cake. Unmold cake by running a hot, dry knife (run knife under hot water, dry blade and use immediately) around the inside edge of pan, then release the latch of springform.

Slice cake with hot, dry knife into 12 servings.

BEACH PICNIC BROWNIES
Heidi Cusick, Cookin' In

Melt the chocolate with the butter in the top of a double boiler. Turn off heat. Stir in sugar. Add eggs and beat well with a wooden spoon. Stir in flour, then add vanilla and nuts.

Pour into a greased and floured 8" x 8" cake pan. Bake in preheated 325 degree oven for 30 minutes. Let cool for 10 minutes before cutting and removing from pan. Wrap while warm to ensure moistness. Makes 16 2-inch brownies.

4 oz. unsweetened chocolate

1/2 cup unsalted butter

1 1/2 cups sugar

4 eggs

Dash salt

1 cup flour

1 cup walnuts, pecans, or almonds, lightly toasted and chopped

THE MODEL BAKERY BROWNIES

In a saucepan, over medium heat, melt butter and add chocolate; stir until melted. In a bowl, beat eggs, sugar, and salt until thick; slowly add melted chocolate and butter. Add flour, vanilla, and espresso. Mix until blended. Fold in walnuts.

Pour into 9" x 9" square pan and bake in 350 degree oven 20-25 minutes until firm. Dust with powdered sugar or frost with chocolate icing, when cool. Makes 12-15 brownies.

6 oz. butter

5 oz. bitter chocolate (five 1 oz. squares)

4 eggs

2 cups sugar

1/2 tsp. salt

1 cup flour

1 tsp. vanilla

1-2 Tbsp. espresso coffee

2 cups chopped walnuts

CHILLED CHOCOLATE TORTONI
Foppiano Vineyards

1 8-oz. pkg semi-sweet chocolate

2/3 cup Karo light or dark corn syrup

2 cups of heavy cream, divided

1 1/2 cups broken chocolate wafers or other crisp cookies

1 cup coarsely chopped walnuts

Line 12 muffin cups with paper liners. In 3 qt saucepan, stir chocolate and corn syrup over low heat just until chocolate melts; remove from heat. Stir in 1/2 cup of heavy cream until blended. Refrigerate 15 minutes or until cool.

Beat remaining cream until soft peaks form; gently stir into chocolate mixture. Stir in cookies and nuts. Spoon into muffin cups.

Freeze 4 to 6 hours or until form. Garnish as desired. Let stand a few minutes before serving. Store covered in freezer up to 1 month. Makes 12.

RASPBERRY & BLACKBERRY BISCUIT PUDDING
Garrett Hall, Vintage Towers

1 cup blackberries, sugared

1 cup raspberries, sugared

6 buttermilk biscuits

2 cups milk

2 cups heavy cream

1 1/2 cups sugar

4 eggs plus 1 yolk

2 Tbsp. Frangelico

2 tsp. real vanilla extract

2 9"-round foil pans, buttered

Arrange 1/4 cup of each berry in pans. Crumble 1 1/2 biscuits over berries in each pan. Repeat with another 1/4 cup layer of berries and another layer of 1 1/2 crumbled biscuits. In large bowl combine eggs, yolk, sugar, Frangelico, and vanilla extract; mix. Add milk and heavy cream. Mix well. Divide liquid equally into each pan. Bake at 325 degrees in water bath for 1 1/2 hours. Cool and refrigerate, serve with whipped cream or fresh fruit.

CHOCOLATE COFFEECAKE
Cafe Beaujolais

For filling, combine all of the filling ingredients in a medium bowl.

To make the cake batter, preheat the oven to 350 degrees. Position a rack in center of the oven. Generously butter the inside of a 10-inch bundt pan and lightly dust with flour. In a medium bowl, stir together the flour, baking powder, baking soda, and salt. Sift together onto a large sheet of waxed paper. In the large bowl of an electric mixer, cream the butter, sugar, and vanilla at medium-high speed for 3 minutes until very light and fluffy. Add the eggs, one at a time, beating well after each addition. At low speed, 1/3 at a time, add the sifted flour mixture alternately with the yogurt, beating after each addition. Beat just until the mixture is smooth. Spread 1/3 of batter over the bottom of the bundt pan. Sprinkle half of filling evenly over the batter. Top with another 1/3 of the batter and sprinkle with the remaining filling. Top with the remaining batter and spread evenly.

Bake for 55 to 60 minutes or until cake tester or toothpick inserted in the center of the cake comes out clean. Let the cake cool in the pan, set on a wire rack, for a few minutes. Invert the cake onto the rack and cool at least 10 minutes before slicing. Dust confectioners' sugar lightly over the top of the cake. Serve warm or at room temperature. Store leftovers in an airtight container.

1/4 cup firmly packed light brown sugar

2 1/2 oz. (about 1/2 cup) finely chopped dried apricots

2 oz. (about 1/2 cup) coarsely chopped walnuts

2 oz. (about 1/3 cup) semi-sweet chocolate chips

2 Tbsp. unsweetened cocoa powder

1 Tbsp. instant coffee powder

2 tsp. ground cinnamon

CAKE BATTER:

2 3/4 cups all purpose flour

1 1/2 tsp. baking powder

1 1/2 tsp. baking soda

1/4 tsp. salt

12 Tbsp. (1 1/2 sticks) unsalted butter, at room temperature

1 1/2 cups granulated sugar

1 tsp. vanilla extract

3 large eggs

2 cups plain yogurt

Confectioners' sugar (for sifting over finished cake)

La Residence

A LUXURY INN
Napa Valley

Exquisite Accommodations ❧ Fireplaces ❧ Pool ❧ Spa

707-253-0337

VERY LITTLE DOUGH CHOCOLATE CHIP COOKIES

1/2 lb. butter
1 cup brown sugar
1 cup white sugar
2 eggs
1 tsp. baking soda
1 tsp. salt
Vanilla
2 1/4 cups flour
1 1/2 cups walnuts
10 oz. Guittard Super Cookie Chips
11 oz. milk chocolate chips
12 oz. semi-sweet chocolate chips

Cream butter, sugar and eggs. Then add soda, salt, and vanilla. Mix in flour and then add chips and nuts. Using a medium ice cream scoop, place on baking sheet, flatten slightly, and then bake for 18 to 19 minutes at 375 degrees.

OPULENT FUDGE CAKE
Geyser Peak Winery

Grease and flour two 9" x 1 1/2" round baking pans. Combine first 3 ingredients in small bowl, set aside. Melt chocolate over medium heat, set aside to cool. In large mixing bowl beat butter on medium speed until creamy (about 30 seconds). Add sugar and vanilla and mix until thoroughly blended. Add eggs, one at a time, beating about 1 minute after each egg. Add cooled chocolate and mix thoroughly. Add in dry ingredients and liquids alternately, beating after each addition. Turn into pans and bake at 350 degrees for about 30 to 40 minutes. Cool 10 minutes and remove from pans.

(A box cake—dark chocolate is best—can be used. Substitute 1 cup wine and 1/4 cup water for the liquid specified in the directions.)

For cream cheese frosting, beat together cream cheese, butter and wine until light and fluffy. Gradually add powdered sugar, beating until smooth. Spread over cooled cake and sprinkle with chopped nuts, if desired.

*Wine available at Geyser Peak Winery Tasting Room

2 cups all-purpose flour

1 1/4 tsp. baking soda

1/2 tsp. salt

2/3 cup butter or margarine

1 3/4 cups sugar

1 tsp. vanilla

2 eggs

3 squares (3 oz.) unsweetened chocolate (melted and cooled)

1 cup Opulence*

1/4 cup cold water

CREAM CHEESE FROSTING

1 pkg. (8oz.) cream cheese

1/2 cup butter or margarine, softened

2 to 3 tsp. Opulence*

3 to 4 cups sifted powdered sugar

1/2 cup finely chopped nuts (optional)

POACHED PEARS IN ZINFANDEL WITH MACAROONS
Chautéau Souverain

4 ripe, but firm, Comise, Bartlett or Bosc pears

3 cups Chateau Souverain Zinfandel

1 1/2 cups sugar

1 lemon (zest and juice)

1/4 cinnamon stick

1 vanilla bean, split in half lengthwise

2 peppercorns

1 clove

1 thyme sprig

4 mint sprigs

MACAROONS

350 grams almonds (blanched and sliced)

350 grams powdered sugar

200 grams egg whites

450 grams powdered sugar

40 grams unsweetened cocoa powder

Mix the Zinfandel, sugar, vanilla bean, spices, herbs, and lemon zest in a sauce pan, bring to a boil and simmer for 5 minutes. Carefully peel, core, and cut the pears in half. Work one at a time, dipping each half in the lemon juice before immediately immersing it in the simmering syrup. Simmer for 8-10 minutes or until a small knife inserted in the middle of the pear meets a slight resistance. Carefully pour everything into a bowl, leave to cool (several hours will do, but overnight is best).

NOTE: The syrup may be used a couple of times.

The recipe for macaroons makes about 30 cookies. The cooking time will vary depending on the oven. (The measurements are in grams—I would not attempt to convert them as the result may not be as successful.) Remember, the macaroons are delicate, both to make and to eat. A smooth, shiny surface and very moist center is the correct appearance.

Finely sift the 350 grams of powdered sugar and combine with the sifted cocoa powder. In a food processor, finely chop the almonds, add the powdered sugar and cocoa mixture to the almonds, mix well. Place the egg whites into a very clean mixing bowl, whip for 30 seconds, then add the 450 grams of powdered sugar. Whip until they are very stiff, sprinkle the mixture in the food processor over the egg whites and fold in gently with a spatula—the mixture should be extremely smooth. Pipe the mixture onto a baking sheet lined with wax paper—even-sized rounds should be piped in staggered rows, about 1" apart. Place in a preheated oven at 350 degrees for 15 minutes (remember, you may have to work out the correct timing for your oven). After the macaroons are cool, they may be kept in an airtight container.

To assemble the dessert, just take out 2 halves of the pears and slice 3/4 of the way up to enable you to fan out the halves. Place the 2 uncut edges of the pears together, strain a little of the syrup over them and garnish with the mint sprig. Serve the macaroons off to the side.

NOTE: Try filling the macaroons with granache to serve with the poached pears, or fill them with raspberry jam by placing two macaroons together.

APPLESAUCE CAKE
Ridenhour Ranch House Inn

Preheat oven to 360 degrees. Grease and flour a 13" x 9" x 2" baking pan (Pyrex works best).

Put all ingredients into large mixing bowl, except for egg whites and 1/2 cup sugar. Beat approximately 7 minutes on medium speed, then 5 minutes on high speed.

Beat egg whites with sugar until very stiff. For best results, chill egg whites and mixing bowl in freezer for a few minutes. Fold egg mixture into batter.

Bake for 65–70 minutes, or until toothpick comes out clean.

2 1/2 cups all-purpose flour

2 cups sugar

1 tsp. baking soda

1 1/2 tsp. baking powder

2 tsp. salt

1 tsp. ground cinnamon

3/4 tsp. ground cloves

3/4 tsp. allspice

2 cups applesauce

1/2 cup melted butter

4 eggs, separated

1/4 cup cold water

1 cup raisins

1 cup walnuts, chopped fine

1 1/2 cups sweet chocolate chips

PANNA DI CAFFE
(Caramelized Espresso Custard)
Michael Ghilarducci, Depot 1870 Restaurant

Beat 5 eggs until fluffy. Slowly add 9 tablespoons sugar, 16 ounces espresso, and 1 tablespoon rum.

Melt 1 cup butter over medium high heat until it melts and turns golden brown, stirring constantly. Pour at once equally into the bottoms of four 8-ounce oven proof souffle dishes or ramekins.

Pour the espresso/egg mixture on top, place in a pan filled with warm water so that the water comes about halfway up the sides of the dishes. Bake 1/2 hour at 350 degrees. Chill. Invert on a fancy serving plate to serve, pouring any caramel remaining in each cup over the custard.

BLOOD ORANGE SORBET
The Restaurant

3 cups blood orange juice

3/4 cup lemon juice

1 1/2 cups Sugar Syrup

1/4 cup Mandarin Napoleon liquor

SUGAR SYRUP

3 cup water

2 1/4 cups sugar

Stir all ingredients together, strain, chill, and freeze in cream freezer, according to manufacturer's directions.

In saucepan, bring 3 cups water and 2 1/4 cups sugar to a boil, simmer for 3–4 minutes, until sugar dissolves. Remove from heat, cool and chill.

This sorbet is full of flavor, very tangy, and the most beautiful deep red color.

Makes 1 1/2 quarts.

TORTA DI MELE
(Custard Apple Tart)
Depot 1870 Restaurant

Make a 12" sweet pastry crust in the tart pan. Pare, core, and slice the apples. Mix well with the cinnamon and 1/2 cup sugar. Arrange in the unbaked crust and bake 25 minutes at 375 degrees. Combine the cream, eggs, and the rest of the sugar. When 25 minutes are up, pour the cream mixture over the apples and bake about 1/2 hour more, until the custard is set. Let cool about 15 minutes, sprinkle with the powdered sugar and serve warm.

One unbaked tart shell crust
4 large apples
3/4 tsp. cinnamon
1/2 cup sugar
2 eggs, beaten
1/2 cup sugar
Powdered sugar

CHAMPAGNE SORBET
Roederer Estate

Combine sugar and water in small saucepan over medium-high heat and stir just until sugar is dissolved. Just before mixture comes to a boil, remove from heat. Cool slightly, cover, and chill.

Combine cold syrup with champagne and lemon zest and blend well. Place in large cake pan and freeze. Beat in food processor until smooth. Add egg whites and mix well. Refreeze in airtight container. About 30 minutes before serving, remove from freezer and place in refrigerator to soften and maximize flavor and texture.

Makes about 8 4-ounce servings.

1 cup water
1 cup sugar
2 cups champagne
Zest of 1 lemon, minced (yellow rind only)
2 egg whites

PINOT NOIR POMEGRANATE SORBET
Greenwood Ridge Vineyards

1 cup Greenwood Ridge Vineyards Pinot Noir

1 cup pomegranate juice (strained)

2 cups water

2 Tbsp. granulated sugar

1/2 cup grapefruit juice (stained)

This simple dessert is perfect after a fish course, or refreshing as a dessert in itself. Follow it with a glass of Anderson Valley Pinot Noir.

Combine 1/2 cup of water and sugar in a saucepan. Bring to a boil and cool to room temperature. Mix together the Pinot Noir, pomegranate juice, grapefruit juice and remaining water. Add the sugar syrup and mix well. Freeze in a shallow pan until solid. Empty the frozen mixture into the food processor. Process on pulse just until the texture is consistent, then freeze again in a covered plastic container. If you have an ice cream maker, follow the manufacturer's directions for sorbet, then transfer to a plastic container. If kept airtight and frozen, the sorbet will last for 3 to 4 days.

6 servings.

Wine was created from the beginning to make men joyful, and not to make men drunk. Wine drunk with moderation is the joy of the soul and the heart.

Ecclesiastes 31:35

PEAR CHAMPAGNE SORBET
Oak Knoll Inn

Simmer all ingredients in a sauce pan until pears are soft and alcohol has evaporated (10-15 minutes). Blend until smooth in a food processor. Let mixture cool. Add 1/2 cup heavy cream and freeze in an ice cream machine.

5 pears, peeled, cored, and cut into cubes

2 cups Domaine Chandon champagne

3/4 cup sugar

1/2 tsp. freshly grated nutmeg

1 tsp. lemon juice

1/2 cup heavy cream

PEACH SORBET
Kenwood Vineyards

Halve and peel the peaches. Remove the pits and slice the peaches into a non-corroding sauce pan. Add the apricots and the Yulupa Chardonnay and cook, covered, over low heat. Stir the fruit often, until heated, approximately 10 to 15 minutes.

Puree the fruit in a food processor fitted with the metal blade. Stir in the sugar until it dissolves. Chill the puree (approximately 3 cups). Stir in the lemon juice to taste.

Freeze according to the directions with your ice cream maker. Makes 1 quart.

1 3/4 lbs. very ripe peaches (Babcock, if available)

1/4 cup dried apricots, thinly sliced

2 Tbsp. Kenwood Yulupa Chardonnay

1/2 cups sugar

Juice of 1/2 medium-sized lemon

RASPBERRY SORBET
Jeanette Stroh, caterer to Parducci Wine Cellars

3 1-lb. packages frozen raspberries (or other berries)
2 cups sugar
1 1/2 cups water
1/3 cup Parducci Zinfandel (optional)

Boil sugar and water together for five minutes to make a simple syrup. Let cool to room temperature. In food processor or blender, puree the frozen fruit and syrup together in batches. Combine pureed batches and add wine. Pour into a 9" x 13" pan. Freeze for 6-8 hours or overnight. (Cover if freezing and storing sorbet for later use.) When completely frozen, remove from freezer and let stand at room temperature for 5-10 minutes. Cut into 1" cubes with knife. Fill fluted champagne glasses with 6-8 cubes each. Garnish with mint leaves. Return to freezer until serving.

Makes 12 generous servings, approximately 78 calories per serving.

Thus, it is proposed that the antioxidant compounds in wine, particularly red wine, exert protective effects that are instrumental in inhibiting oxidative reactions involved in artherogenesis and thrombosis.

Joseph E. Kinsella, Ph.D., Dean, College of Agricultural and Environmental Sciences, University of California, Davis

INDEX

*I wonder often what the vintners buy one half
so precious as the stuff they sell*

Omar Khayyam (1048–1122)

SPECIAL MENUS

BABY LETTUCE SALAD WITH PRAWNS & GRAPEFRUIT 7
CARAMELIZED ONION TARTE TATIN 2
CHOCOLATE SORBET 5
CURRIED CHICKEN BREASTS 11
PEAR SORBET 5
POACHED PEARS IN WINE CREAM WITH RASPBERRIES 9
RASPBERRY MILKSHAKE IN A CHOCOLATE BAG 4
RICE SALAD 11
SALTIMBOCCA ALLA ROMA 8
SPICY FLORIDA ROCK SHRIMP RISOTTO 3

APPETIZERS

ALI-OLI 21
BAKED CHEESE & SUN-DRIED TOMATO ROUNDS 19
GOAT CHEESE CAKE 14
MACCALLUM HOUSE MUSHROOMS 17
MAPLE-BACON PANCAKES 22
MUSHROOMS IN GARLIC SAUCE 20
PROSCIUTTO WILD MUSHROOM BREAD 18
ROMESCO 21
SEAFOOD IN PHYLLO DOUGH 16
SMOKED SALMON CHEESECAKE 19
SPICY APRICOT-GINGER APPETIZER 14
SUN-DRIED TOMATO & CHEESE HORS D'OEUVRE 15

BREAKFAST

BREAD PUDDING WITH WHISKEY SAUCE 46
BROCCOLI CHEESE PUFFS 43
CARAMELIZED APPLESAUCE 40
CLASSIC CREAM SCONES 37
COFFEE CAN BREAD 33
CRAB CREPE FILLING 25
EGGS FLORENTINE 27
FRITTATA ALLA VEDURA 32
GERMAN PANCAKES 41
GOLDEN ORANGE PANCAKES 28
HEAVENLY PUMPKIN GEMS 30
HOT APPLE OATMEAL CEREAL 44
HUEVOS RANCHEROS 39
HUEVOS WHITEGATE 27
JOHN DOUGHERTY HOUSE SCONES 35

LEMON PANCAKES	29
MARGARET PARDUCCI'S ZUCCHINI PANCAKES	43
NAME THAT MUFFIN	38
OLE'S SWEDISH HOTCAKES	32
ORANGE MARMALADE MUFFINS	24
OVERNIGHT SOUR DOUGH FRENCH TOAST	33
PEACH CREAM CHEESE CREPES	35
POPPY SEED TEA CAKE	34
PUFFY FRUIT OMELET	31
SALSA-CHEESE OMELET	26
SOUTH OF THE BORDER FRITTATA	42
SPICED APPLE CIDER	41
SPINACH POTATO PIE	26
SPINACH-MUSHROOM FETA FILLOS	45
STUFFED BAKED PEARS	36
WHOLE WHEAT SCONES	34
ZUCCHINI BREAD	25
ZUCCHINI QUICHE	47

SOUPS AND SALADS

AUSTRALIAN PIE FLOATER	58
CHESTNUT SOUP	61
CREAMY RED BELL PEPPER SOUP	52
FRESH ASPARAGUS SOUP	52
GOLDEN POTATO SOUP	51
PRAWN SALAD WITH ROAST PEPPERS	56
ROASTED PUMPKIN RISOTTO WITH FRESH SAGE	55
ROY'S SALMON SALAD	53
SONOMA VALLEY SALAD FOR TWO	60
STEAK SALAD WITH BLUE CHEESE DRESSING	54
THICK PEA AND HAM SOUP	59
TOMATO SOUP WITH GRILLED SEA SCALLOPS AND CHERVIL	50
VEGETARIAN BLACK BEAN SOUP	51
WARM CALAMARI SERVED IN A WHITE BEAN VINAIGRETTE	57
WARM CHICKEN SAUSAGE AND POTATO SALAD	63
WARM SPINACH SALAD WITH SCALLOPS	62

ENTREES

BARBECUED TROUT	74
BLACK BEAN CHILE	110
BUTTERFLIED FILET OF BEEF WITH HERBS	112
BUTTERMILK PECAN CHICKEN BREAST	86
CASSOULET FROM PUY	111

CHARDONNAY STEAMED CLAMS	73
CHICKEN BREAST WITH BLEU CHEESE IN A ROSEMARY PEAR SAUCE	85
COQUILLE ST. JACQUE	67
CORNISH GAME HENS GLAZED WITH PEPPER ORANGE SAUCE	81
COUNTRY CHICKEN PICCATA	87
FETTUCCINE WITH CHICKEN	78
FETTUCCINE, CHICKEN BREAST AND MUSHROOMS IN WHITE SAUCE	75
FETTUCINE ALFREDO	88
FOPPIANO CHRISTMAS RAVIOLI	107
GRATIN OF POLENTA, TOMATO FONDUE & SONOMA JACK	97
GRILLED BREAST OF CHICKEN WITH ORANGE-APRICOT GLAZE	81
GRILLED CHICKEN BREAST TOPPED WITH SUN-DRIED TOMATO PESTO	83
GRILLED CHICKEN BREAST WITH MERLOT SAUCE	87
GRILLED MEDALLIONS OF VENISON WITH BLACKBERRY SAGE SAUCE	96
GRILLED OPA WITH ROASTED TOMATO, PECAN VINAIGRETTE	66
HASENPFEFFER	115
HOLIDAY ROAST	113
HOT PASTA PRIMAVERA	108
HOT PEPPER GLAZE	82
ITALIAN BAKED VEGETABLES	69
JIM'S PASTA	102
LAMB WITH CILANTRO/CUMIN CRUST	95
LEG OF LAMB WITH MUSTARD AND HERBS	94
ORANGE-COATED PORK LOINS	106
PASTA ALL'ARRABBIATA	104
PASTA BANDIERA	101
PASTA PUTTANESCA FRESCA	105
PASTA WITH PEPERONATA SAUCE	109
POACHED TROUT	74
POLENTA CASSEROLE	90
POPPY HONEY CHICKEN	82
PRAWNS BORDELAISE	68
RALO'S QUICK AND EASY VERSATILE SAUCE	100
RAVIOLI IN A LEMON CREAM SAUCE	103
RISOTTO WITH GRILLED FENNEL & CHATEAU CURED SALMON	70
ROASTED GAME HENS ZINFANDEL	80
SALMON AU BEURRE D'ESHALOTES	72

SALMON WRAPPED IN LETTUCE LEAVES	73
SAVORY STEAKS WITH SUN-DRIED TOMATO TOPPING	114
SCALLOPED YAMS WITH PECANS	99
STUFFED GUINEA FOWL	76
THAI-STYLE CASHEW CHICKEN	79
TRADITIONAL ROAST GOOSE	84
TRENTADUE TOURNEDOS	92
VEAL DIJONNAISE (Sauteed Veal with Mustard Sauce)	93
VITELLO CON FUNGHI E CREAMAS (Veal)	91
WILD RICE SAGE DRESSING	98
ZINFANDEL FENNEL TOMATO SAUCE	89

DESSERTS

APPLESAUCE CAKE	133
BEACH PICNIC BROWNIES	127
BLOOD ORANGE SORBET	134
BOURBON AND KENWOOD WALNUT TART	120
CHAMPAGNE SORBET	135
CHILLED CHOCOLATE TORTONI	128
CHOCOLATE COFFEECAKE	129
CHOCOLATE FRANGELICO CHEESECAKE	118
CHOCOLATE MACADAMIA NUT PIE	125
CHOCOLATE SILK	126
FRUIT TART WITH NUT CRUST	124
LEMON CHIFFON STRAWBERRY SAUCE	123
MAGIC CHOCOLATE CAKE	116
OPULENT FUDGE CAKE	131
PANNA DI CAFFE	134
PEACH SORBET	137
PEAR CHAMPAGNE SORBET	137
PINOT NOIR POMEGRANATE SORBET	136
POACHED PEARS IN ZINFANDEL WITH MACAROONS	132
RASPBERRY & BLACKBERRY BISCUIT PUDDING	128
RASPBERRY SORBET	138
RUSSIAN CREAM WITH WILD HUCKLEBERRIES	121
SPA COFFEE ICE CREAM	122
SWEDISH APPLE CAKE	121
THE MODEL BAKERY BROWNIES	127
TIRAMI SU (Lift Me Up)	119
TORTA DI MELE	135
VERY LITTLE DOUGH CHOCOLATE CHIP COOKIES	130

143

LIST OF CONTRIBUTORS

ALICE WATERS 112
BANDIERA WINERY 14, 81, 98-99, 114
BISTRO RALPH 66
BRAVA TERRACE 50, 111
CAFE BEAUJOLAIS 38-40, 110, 113, 129
CANYON ROAD 100-101
CAZANOMA LODGE 115
CHATEAU SOUVERAIN 70, 132
CHATEAU ST. JEAN 14
CHEZ OVERNIGHT & OVERNIGHT 52
CHOCOLATE MOOSE CAFE 63
DEHAVEN VALLEY FARM 16
DEPOT 1870 RESTAURANT 32, 134-135
DOMAINE CHANDON 2-5,
EASTSIDE OYSTER BAR & GRILL 120
EQUUS RESTAURANT 60
FARMHOUSE INN 37, 125
FENSALDEN INN 22, 24-26
FETZER VINEYARDS 84, 96
FOPPIANO 106-107, 109, 128
FOUNTAINGROVE INN 83
FRAMPTON HOUSE BED & BREAKFAST 33
GEYSER PEAK WINERY 15, 58, 59, 73, 131
GLORIA FERRER CHAMPAGNE CELLARS 20, 21
GOWAN'S OAK TREE 121
GREENWOOD RIDGE VINEYARDS 89, 136
HAMBURGER RANCH 75
HEIDI CUSICK, "COOKIN' IN" 124, 127
HIGHLAND DELL INN 34, 41
HOT PEPPER JELLY CO. 46, 81-82
INN AT OCCIDENTAL 61
INN ON CEDAR STREET 42
ITALIAN AFFAIR 88, 91
J. PEDRONELLI WINERY 69, 119
JOHN ASH & CO. 76, 77
JOHN DOUGHERTY HOUSE 35, 65
KENWOOD WINERY 18, 137

CONTRIBUTORS

LA GARE FRENCH RESTAURANT	68, 72, 93
LA RESIDENCE	130
LANDMARK VINEYARDS	53, 74
LEDFORD HOUSE RESTAURANT	85, 94
LINCOLN AVE. GRILL	87
LISA HEMMENWAY'S	34
LITTLE RIVER INN	32
MACCALLUM HOUSE RESTAURANT	17, 118
MEADOWOOD	56, 57
MODEL BAKERY	127
OAK KNOLL INN	36, 137
PARDUCCI WINERY	33, 43, 138
PETER RABBIT'S CHOCOLATE FACTORY	116
PLAZA GRILL	108
PUDDING CREEK INN	35
RAYMOND VINEYARDS & CELLAR	7-9
RESTAURANT, THE	52, 78-79, 102, 126, 134
RIDENHOUR RANCH HOUSE INN	133
RISTORANTE PIATTI	103
RISTORANTE SIENA	105
ROEDERER ESTATE	135
SANDPIPER HOUSE INN	28-31
SCHARFFENBERGER CELLARS	10-11
SEBASTIANI WINERY	90
SIMI WINERY	54, 55, 95
SONOMA CHEESE FACTORY	19, 97
SONOMA MISSION INN & SPA	73, 122-123
SPRING STREET RESTAURANT	51, 86
ST. FRANCIS VINEYARDS	87
SUTTER HOME	80
TIDES, THE	19
TRENTADUE WINERY	92, 104
VINTAGE TOWERS	128
WERMUTH WINERY	62
WHALE WATCH INN,	44-45
WHARF, THE	67
WHITEGATE INN	27, 41, 43, 47, 121

SUBSCRIBE
to the Wine Country

SEMI ANNUAL

The essential resource guide for every Wine Country visitor. Discover the small towns, the back roads leading to undiscovered wineries and natural wonders, the special shops with unique treasures to take home. Enjoy the recipes shared by renowned Wine Country chefs. From the Carneros Wine Region, which bonds Napa and Sonoma Counties, to the Mendocino Coast, all the North Coast Region's treasures are colorfully revealed in Steppin' Out Magazine.

Send this application with $5 for each subscription to:

Steppin Out

P.O. Box 1458 • Fort Bragg, CA 95437

ONE FOR YOU:

Name _____
Address _____
City _____ State _____ Zip _____

AND ONE FOR A FRIEND:

Name _____
Address _____
City _____ State _____ Zip _____

A SPECIAL FEATURE:
WINE COUNTRY RECIPES

and

Steppin Out
MAGAZINE

- *152 chosen recipes from noted winemakers, innkeepers and chefs*
- *Suggestions on food & wine pairings*
- *Complete menu ideas highlighting recipes*
- *Two issues of Steppin' Out Magazine*

To order, send $7.95 (includes tax, shipping and handling), or a one-year subscription & cookbook for the featured price of $12.00, all charges inclusive, to:

Francis Publications
P.O. Box 1458 • Fort Bragg, CA 95437

Please send to:
- ☐ Name _____
  Address _____
  _____

Gifts:
- ☐ Name _____
  Address _____
  _____

- ☐ Name _____
  Address _____
  _____

Amount Enclosed _____